Cecil Collins

AF328487

BRIAN KEEBLE

Cecil Collins

The Artist as Writer and Image Maker

GOLGONOOZA PRESS

First published by
Golgonooza Press
3 Cambridge Drive
Ipswich, IP2 9EP

The right of Brian Keeble to be identified
as the author of the work has been asserted
by him in accordance with the Copyright,
Designs and Patents Act 1988

Copyright © Brian Keeble 2009
All Cecil Collins material copyright © Tate, London, 2009

All rights reserved. No part of this book
may be reproduced or transmitted in any form
or by any means, electronic or mechanical,
without prior permission in writing
from the copyright holder.

British Library Cataloguing in Publication Data
A catalogue record of this book is available
from the British Library

ISBN 978 0 903880 83 1

Typeset by Agnesi Text, Hadleigh
Printed by Cloister Press, Cambridge

For Elizabeth

In Remembrance

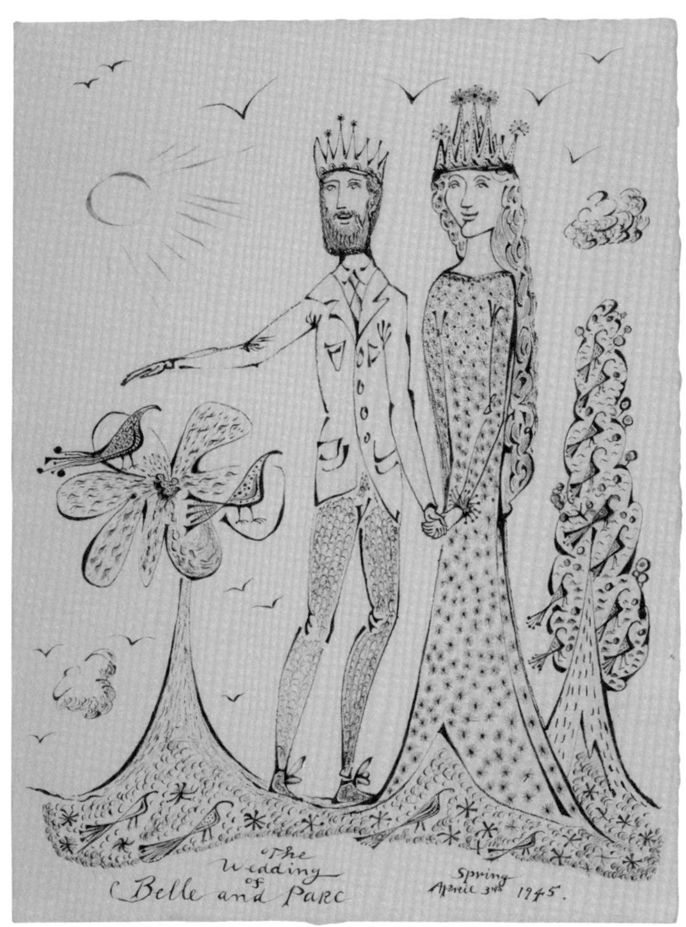

The Wedding of Belle and Parc 1945
pencil, ink and watercolour on paper, 38 × 280

Contents

INTRODUCTION

I have always been concerned with art as metaphysical experience, and in my painting I have continued to explore this metaphysical experience as poetic consciousness. A picture lives on many different levels at once: it is an interpenetration of different planes of reality; it cannot be analysed or anatomized into single levels, because one level can be understood only in the light of other levels. The reality of the picture can be realized only as a total experience.

Let these words, written towards the end of the artist's life and as if to summarize his whole intention, be the point of orientation in all that follows.

CECIL COLLINS was born into a world on the brink of discovering non-representational art, with its new freedom, a freedom that initiated new challenges, demands and responsibilities. For several centuries Western art had accepted the world of natural appearances as the arbiter of pictorial content. This certainty as to what art should re-present was no longer to go unchallenged. The advent of abstraction gave to the artist a spectrum of images ranging from natural appearances *per se* – though with some degree of stylistic distortion – all the way to pure abstraction where the substance of pictorial content is carried by line, mass, colour, shape, or simply the medium itself. This sudden irruption of new expressive possibilities proved sufficient for those artists for whom the contours of reality are defined by the world of nature on the one hand and the conceptual matter of thought itself on the other.

For the artist who sees beyond these dualistic limitations such stylistic boundaries are insufficient. For the visionary artist who has, by virtue of an intuitive gift of imagination, some intimations of the ineffable unity that encompasses (and makes possible) these two 'faces' of reality (appearances and mental images) this insufficiency poses a deep-seated problem. What exactly is to be the authentic pictorial language that could give adequate expression to that wholeness of vision that is firmly rooted in metaphysical experience? This was the problem that faced Collins at the start of his career.

When such words as 'mystical' and 'visionary' are linked to Collins's art what is being acknowledged, whether consciously or not, is that his art expresses a sensibility that has a natural awareness of the supra-natural. Collins had this awareness from the beginning. But in the modern world, especially the world of modern art, this awareness is rare and in any case quite foreign to what is usually admitted as art, both as a general conception and as a valid field of artistic expression. Burdened as he is by what has been called his agnostic reflex, it is not part of modern man's intuitive sense of the condition that makes up the 'real' to feel himself to be an amphibious creation, inhabiting quite naturally and as a unified whole, noumenal and phenomenal orders of reality. From the point of view of the 'metaphysical experience' that Collins speaks of these orders are fused but not confused, and in so far as they can be considered as separate from one another therein resides an imperative, since what is implied by this 'separation' is the need to recognize that man naturally seeks the satisfactions of happiness, beauty and truth. Which is to say, man naturally desires the divine substance in so far as he wishes to find rest in wholeness of being.

All the traditions that Collins would have accepted as spiritually authentic have taught that, however he might be deceived or distracted, none the less, it is man's nature to aspire to a knowledge of what absolutely *is*. Collins, in both his writings and his pictures, always acknowledges this aspirational imperative. It underpinned all he did, even though at times he failed to achieve an adequate symbolic language with which to express it. Some of his early works of the 1930s are weakened by a rather affected arrangement of loosely related symbols (as in *Thy Thoughts O Life*, plate 3) and in some later periods, he became overly absorbed in the formal gestures of the creative process itself, as in his *Lyric Landscape* of 1967 (plate 23).

Collins's singular achievement as an artist rests upon his attempt to preserve the continuity between the natural and the supra-natural, the human and the Divine, by means of beauty, at a time when such an order of vision was seldom acknowledged. Few of his statements about art make sense if considered apart from the inclusive context of this aspirational imperative, as witness his avowed concern with 'metaphysical experience', and his belief that, through the imaginative unity of 'poetic consciousness', his pictures live at once in the 'interpenetration of different planes of reality'.

From early in his life it seems likely that the future painter had, not so much a revelatory moment as a steadily developing intuitive awareness of the divine origin and unity of things. During the decade of the thirties his main preoccupation was to consider the meaning of this imaginative predisposition towards the Divine, as well as evolving a pictorial symbolism that was at once aesthetically satisfying and symbolically cogent. In this he was aided as much by his reading of the scriptures and certain mystics – Traherne and Eckhart were central to this development – as he was by the example of many earlier artists. No artist before him quite shared the trajectory of his artistic ambition, to express through colour, line, light and symbolic characterization, and through modes of love and joy, the motion towards the Divine; a motion in which art can be said to embody the 'redeeming context', as he called it, of the very nature of consciousness itself.

This is not to say that Collins ignored the stylistic innovations of modernism, even if he did reject the intellectual and artistic premisses on which those innovations were founded. A glance at a good many of his pictures will confirm that he absorbed and then made use of many of the stylistic features of his contemporaries. No artist rejects entirely, even if it were possible, the artistic conventions of his own age, for they are unwittingly absorbed before the arrival of any deliberation as to what might constitute one's own artistic style. None the less, Collins was to reject naturalistic imagery as decisively as he also rejected the sterile formalism of those rational 'mental diagrams', as he called them, that are the content of much abstract art. But there were solid grounds for this rejection.

From the point of view of the 'metaphysical experience' the artist espoused, the various 'isms' of the evolution of modernism were no more than a development that had begun centuries earlier. From the Renaissance the continuous mutation of artistic styles in European art represented an attempt to attach pictorial content to the perception of natural appearances, assuming the objects so perceived to be the very stuff of reality. The advent of abstraction in the first decade of the twentieth century did not really challenge this assumption; it merely invited the artist to internalize pictorial content in order to recast it on the basis of a chosen subjective/artistic agenda. But from the standpoint of one who wishes to base his art on the truth that is, in Collins's words, 'universal and eternal, above and beyond the world of intellect and the senses' (103),* this is a form of deception. It is to limit reality to 'created' nature and to withhold the function of 'creative' nature (God's imaginative wisdom), in the disclosure of the wholeness of the Divine Reality. For Collins this truncation in the way we comprehend reality is not compensated for by an appeal to the visual resources of non-representational forms. Even though they are not depicted 'naturalistically', none the less, when it comes to grasping the import of the images we see in Collins's pictures, a fundamental distinction has to be made.

The painter's intention is not, as is the case with many of his contemporaries (such as Paul Nash and Graham Sutherland, for instance), to render any 'hidden qualities' of natural appearances, if by that is meant simply to express aesthetic nuances beyond what is grasped by corporeal vision; such nuances as might be felt at the level of private emotion or personal fantasy. Collins's intention is far more cosmological. For this painter, the true aim of art is to facilitate the spiritual impulse of the soul towards the Divine Unity, a unity that must, by definition, and on pain of otherwise effecting an irresolvable dualism, be inclusive of the natural world. For Collins, the image that draws upon natural appearances (but which does not necessarily imitate them) ought to be the visual correspondence of a higher state of being since, as it were, it is the likeness of the Divine Imagination shaped to lift the spectator beyond the world of the senses, without negating the senses or the world it is their nature to apprehend.

* Bracketed figures following all quotations are page references to Cecil Collins, *The Vision of the Fool and other writings*, second, enlarged edition, Golgonooza Press, Ipswich, 2002.

Collins certainly saw that from the perspective of what absolutely *is*, the world of created nature is an illusion. He also understood that to dispense with its forms in favour of images generated by the rational mind brings us no closer to understanding the Reality in respect of which they are illusory. 'God', as he pointed out, 'is the stillness, the solitude, the nothingness in which all forms die and are born again.' (35) The all-comprehending revelation of the Real necessitates nothing less than the full and unconditional 'actualization of soul'–an awakening of unconditional consciousness that true aesthetic experience must fulfil. In this condition the soul manifests the likenesses that form the creation as symbols which themselves act out the role of that ultimate illusion; to make evident the divine play that dances at the centre of each and every atom of the creation. Such a comprehensive artistic vision was without precedent in the art of his time and set Collins apart from his contemporaries.

Like William Blake and Samuel Palmer before him, Collins was not destined to be widely appreciated in his lifetime, the spirituality of his vision being too radical for the bodily centred responses of a materialistic age. Might we see in this rejection a trace of unconscious retribution, seeing that the painter's vision was deeply subversive of many of the cultural pretensions of his contemporaries?

When the poet Kathleen Raine asked him if he actually saw the Angels he painted, the artist replied, 'I paint so that I can see them.' The directional impulse of this response should not escape us when we come to contemplate his images. They are certainly not understood if we approach them through the disfiguring eyes of the modernist aesthetic. In addition, we must ask why, and on what terms, certain of his works do not fulfil the promise of his philosophy.

The Fool, the Angel, the Sybil and their companions exist to articulate, in the artist's words, the 'visual music of the kingdom of the imagination'. We must therefore engage with them spiritually. Precisely because of the discipline imposed on the painter and the viewer by the need to re-cognize the fact that 'poetic consciousness' may serve as a mirror to the Divine, we see that the painter was not free to approach his art as if picture-making is a matter of exploring the pictorial values of space, colour, mass, line and texture, a concept so dear to the agenda of the modernist aesthetic.

Even if we readily concede that from the standpoint of the modernist view an exploration of the full range of possibilities of the creative act has seemed a necessary and natural development, that does not permit us to forget that the creative act in itself must be directed towards something other than simply giving expression to creativity as such. We do not look at a picture merely to have our optical nerve-ends stimulated. Without the mind being present the eye is open to no purpose, as Eckhart pointed out. We actually look with the mind's eye taking in a complexity of resonances that relate simultaneously to multiple lines of reference: visual, historical, cultural, psychological and spiritual, not to mention many facets of context that arise from personal associations. The mind demands that these different levels cohere in a unified whole. Each of the levels may well deal with relative truths, but the mind knows of its nature that relativities are only so in respect of the Absolute, of which it is the created reflection. This intuitive 'ground' is unknowable as a distinct object of knowledge, but to the extent it is potentially present in the full realization of 'poetic consciousness' it is the focal point and summit of true artistic achievement from Collins's point of view.

Such a perspective as Collins propounded is simply alien and lost to an art that is content to have the manifestation of creative energy as its goal. For all that a certain vivacity of execution, a vibrancy of colour, the spontaneity of gesture in the rendering of forms (such as, it must be admitted, are present in works by Collins – in his *Lyrical Landscape*, for example – the overall effect is of the seeking of a freedom that, in the final analysis, is incoherent and destructive of the unity of experience Collins's vision demands. That ineffable, intuitive illumination that is the evocation of a hidden reality is, ultimately, only realizable in and through the 'illusory' likeness of the world of our common sensory experience. 'I believe that the Divine Reality should be reflected in the wholeness of human experience, in nature and in man himself . . . in an insect, in an ant, in a fly on the window pane, in a speck of dust,' (170) as Collins himself put it. Not all of his pictures live up to that demanding belief.

The logic of the painter's philosophy, articulated so clearly in his writings, is that the Fool, the Angel, Pilgrim, Sybil and their like must in some measure *be* what they depict rather than seem to be merely illustrative, figurative substitutes for these inhabitants of the 'kingdom of the imagination'. We will return to this question. At their best, that is, at their most fully realized they pre-figure states of being that the viewer, prompted by the image, must *be*. The viewer must bring to the experience of them the soul's activated presence as the picture's witness. It is surely inescapable that the philosophy of art, so painstakingly recorded in the artist's writings over many years, contains integral criteria of validity when it comes to distinguishing between 'the wrought image to be participated in by contemplation' on the one hand, and what drives 'the artist [and the spectator] to disintegrate into nothingness' on the other. (171–2)

This whole book has been planned as a supplement to my edition of Cecil Collins's writings, collected in *The Vision of the Fool and other writings* (2002). I have not, therefore, repeated illustrations included in that volume or, indeed, in any other publication on the artist, although some have appeared in limited-circulation dealers' and gallery catalogues. Beyond the obvious status of availability I have tried to source, as far as possible, works from all periods which, in effect, also means in the full range of styles and variety of media adopted by the artist throughout his career. With these criteria in mind I have also tried to include the best works available to me. It is not a coincidence that there are many works from the 1940s, the artist's most creative decade. I have also duplicated themes – the two pictures of a Fool carrying a Child, and the two Vases of Flowers – to show his frequent habit of repeating while recasting pictorial themes.

I include here only one example of the works that are very freely executed and are predominantly abstract. This decision has everything to do with my reservation as to the ultimate significance of such works. My reasoning in this matter will, I hope, become clear as this essay proceeds. There is no doubt that, from time to time, Collins felt the need to release himself from an increasingly elaborate formality of execution. It does not seem to me that this necessarily brings corresponding rewards for the viewer. I have seen, in my researches, works of such casual execution, images all but totally abstract, that one could scarcely believe might have come from the same hand, eye and mind that executed, say, *The Invocation* of 1944. Indeed, they might have been executed by any one of a dozen artists of the period.

In so far as this is a supplement to the earlier volume, I must beg the reader's indulgence in referring to the texts and plates in *Vision of the Fool*. When a plate in *Vision* is referred to the bracketed reference becomes (*V*. plate *x*). Plates referred to in this volume are given as (plate *x*). In some cases it has not been possible to identify the details of a picture. For ease of reference I have placed an speculative information in square brackets. The author would welcome any missing details should any reader possess them. The plates are arranged in alphabetical order. Sizes are in centimetres, depth followed by width.

The Artist as Writer

Weak men try to escape from Eternity.
Strong men try to escape from Time. (133)

There are many reasons why an artist might turn to being a writer. A gift for poetry or fiction might beckon. Perhaps an autobiography or some polemical issue becomes an imperative. In our time the chief reason might be sought in an historical development.

Since the rise of individualism in the Renaissance and its subsequent evolution over succeeding centuries, a widening gulf has opened up between the artist and his audience. The position of the artist in society has moved from that of being an artisan responsible to a patron to that of being a creative entrepreneur who operates freely in the market place as talent, taste and fashion permit. As Collins has written, 'All art since the Renaissance has moved into the position of being a manifestation of the vested interests of the ego.' (127) So much is this the case that today the artist can seldom depend on finding among his audience an implied background of shared cultural and artistic values held in common. The position of the artist in society is a problem that occupied Collins all his life: and with good reason. As his writings reveal, he was no different from any of his contemporaries in feeling the need to stake out the territory, the 'theatre' as he came to call it, on which his art was to be enacted. As we shall see, there are compelling reasons why, and on what terms, he was the 'patron' of his own work.

. . . the artist at the present time has no agreed language with which to communicate. In the great civilisations of the past this language, being essentially religious, was a canonic language, it was given to him, handed on to him. His patron called forth from him what he required and he gave it, and he knew he would find happiness of service, which is very different from self-expression.

Today the artist has to create his own language, be his own patron, explain *why* he is a patron. On him alone falls the responsibility that should be shared by the whole of civilisation.' (119)

Every now and then an artist emerges whose destiny it seems to be to question the very foundations on which the cultural values of his own time rest. William Blake was clearly one such. No doubt in part spurred on by Blake's example, Cecil Collins was another. In his well-known manifesto, *The Vision of the Fool* (1944), he states his belief that 'the aesthetic conscience of mankind in most parts of the western world is in general undeveloped' so that 'the positon of the artist in society has become more and more impossible'. (93) No wonder, then, that the beleagured modern artist has need of the pen to defend and explain his intentions. In the case of Collins there is more to it than that. These writings are evidently part of a process that was necessary for the artist; to objectify first in order to subsequently assimilate spiritually.

Not all of Collins's writings are meant to 'explain' his position. It seems likely that at least until the 1940s he thought himself to be as much poet as painter. In 1938 his friend Peter Goffin sent a collection of the artist's poems to T. S. Eliot at Fabers. Rejecting them, Eliot none the less praised their unity of personality and considerable sensibility, while noting their failure to become objective artifacts free from the emotion which had inspired them. Such evidence as has so far come to light suggests Collins did indeed have a considerable poetic sensibility and that this found expression in poetry over a number of years. But it was not only in the formalities of poem-making that this aspect of his creative sensibility found expression. The two collections of Meditations, *The Sceptred Bone and Flower* of 1936 and 1937, were likely compiled from notebooks written in his late 20s.

Many of these Meditations, especially in the First Book, are short passages of poetic prose. That is to say, they seek to communicate their content through the emotional tone and nuance of image and metaphor as much as by didactic thesis and argument. Here, subtlety of mood is everything so that the sympathetic reader is brought into the emotional resonances evoked by each passage. By this means the contours of discrete objects that make up the world of everyday perception begin to seem less divisive, so that the reader's consciousness discovers a subtle affinity with the unity and interrelatedness of things.

Such entries as this, for instance, from Book Two of *The Sceptred Bone and Flower*, are at one and the same time indissolubly poetry, invocation and a declaration of the artist's intent:

> The Love! The Love!
> I see it in the movement of the clouds, the moving of the grass; in
> the dust of the roads, the leaves and branches of the trees, In the
> globules of the rain. (49)

Such a passage certainly exemplifies Collins's confession in a passage from a further set of Meditations (*Hymn of Life*, 1939–1955, but possibly written at the same time): 'My way to God is through the devotion of poetic imagination'. (55)

Another passage from the same work and, again, perhaps written at the same time, vividly presents the artist's poetic method 'at work':

> Now, I can gaze at the beautiful nakedness of stones, put my fore-
> head against the rough bark of the trees, and feel the soft girl
> thigh feeling of leaves, and hear after the waves have fallen upon
> the shore, the hollow eternal sound echoing inward and away
> further and further mingling at a great distance inside of me,
> until it is already among the voices of other kingdoms. (56)

As to how this process of emotional assimilation relates to the images of Collins's visual art, we might recall that the pencil drawing *Bird Singing in a Tree* of 1944 relates directly to an experience recorded in these Meditations. 'The other day I saw and heard a bird singing on the branch of a tree, and suddenly realised that the tree was the shape of the bird's song, they were one.' (56)

It is a distinguishing mark of these Meditations that they possess a profoundly integrated compound of poetic and didactic modes of expression. This may well give us a clue as to why Collins did not develop as a poet. And we must remember the limited evidence we have of his poetic achievement, comprising only the nineteen poems published as *In the Solitude of this Land* in 1981, but originating as far back as the 1940s.

The main weakness of the poems is their frequent inability to fix the flow of images into a coherent, imaginative reality. Evocative as individual lines and images are, all too often there seems to be no discernible undertow of intelligibility that allows us to comprehend why one image follows another – as in these lines, for instance, from the fourth poem of the collection:

> Stillness, stillness.
> Turn a brow of loneliness,
> a glance of stillness
> upon the jewelled scourge of streets.
>
> Perfumed dark
> the wreath of utterance,
> the enigmatic wine,
> the sceptre . . .. (177)

That said, at their best, Collins the poet could rise to such as this, the penultimate poem of the sequence.

> What have you hidden Darkness?
> Light, what have you revealed?
> old and familiar
> the desolate ground,
> the bright buds
> small tears of a new life,
> fresh seeds
> of a young and luminous Dawn,
> Persephone's feet
> pale from the shadowy river
> of Hell. (185)

This partial failure of the poems is largely absent from the poetic prose of the Meditations, where the burden of coherence is provided by an intuitive thesis that directs the intelligence towards the wider context of the artist's visionary sensibility.

This visionary sense Collins seems to have possessed from very early in his life. Just as Blake, in one of his earliest works, *All Religions Are One* (etched about 1788), had arrived at a formulation of the *religio perennis* – the idea that a single body of transcendent metaphysical truth underlies all religions – so Collins in the First Book of *The Sceptred Bone and Flower*, expounds the related Vedantic teaching that 'God is the only Self that really exists, all creatures are worlds expressed by that Self.' (34) Nothing that Collins wrote or painted offers a contradiction to this moment of realisation. Indeed, much of the underlying thought running through all the Meditations echoes traditional metaphysical doctrine – but filtered, as it were, through Collins's specific visionary sensibility and thereby given a flavour and colouring uniquely his. One has the impression that all his thought and reading was a confirmation, by way of exploration, of traditional wisdom; from the scriptures of the sacred traditions, poets, mystics and saints and in his later years the writings of A. K. Coomaraswamy and Titus Burckhardt in particular. Again and again we find in Collins's Meditations the resonances of the eternal wisdom spoken from an intuitive apprehension of their inner reality. We must note, too, how often they possess an awareness of the dimension of paradox that necessarily accompanies any attempt to formulate how it is that empirical and mystical worlds of awareness are folded one within the other.

Man has the voices of all Kingdoms in him. (47)

Our life of the five senses is a spark struck by infinite energies
upon the limitations of space and time. (34)

Absence of life is the mercy of life for it creates the desire for life.
(53)

The world has hurt the truth,
and now the truth hurts the world. (62)

Renounce existence for the sake of life. (66)

While it is certainly necessary to acknowledge the poetic colouring in Collins's writings, especially the earlier texts, we must not to lose sight of the fact that they also contained, from the beginning, a strong and determined prescriptive element. The earliest of his published texts was the brief *Foreword* he wrote for the catalogue of his first one-man exhibition in 1935. This is nothing if not a gauntlet thrown down as a challenge to the materialistic assumptions of his contemporaries.

This challenge relates to another theme that always preoccupied him, a theme integral to his visionary perceptions: to examine and lay bare the spiritual impoverishment of the cultural premises of his age. This component of his thinking might justifiably be said to be the chief reason Collins wrote at all in the latter part of his career.

As one might expect under the circumstances, this 'manifesto' (for it amounts to that) was as uncompromising as it was brief. It ends:

> There must be in the world a spiritual revolution NOW. A
>   spiritual revolution
> is the movement of the human consciousness from the ideas
>   of fear and desire,
> victory and defeat, courage and cowardice, possessions – on to the
>   idea of
> intelligence which is humility.
> All force is evil.
> Intelligence is divine.
> All mass revolutions are not action – but reaction.
> Revolution begins in you.
> These are not original ideas, but eternal values. (30)

We also find in this short work a passage that is, in effect, not only a description of the artist's intent at the time but also a foreshadowing of later achievement:

> My works are visual music of the kingdoms of the imagination.
> There is in all human beings a secret, personal life – untouched,
> protected – won from communal life; and of which all public life
> is the enemy. It is this sensitive life which my art is created to feed
> and sustain, this real life deep in each person. Thus my art is truly
> functional. (29)

From Collins's likening of his art to that of a visual music of imaginative reality we understand his subsequent iconography and pictorial techniques. From his claim that his images are 'truly functional' we understand his unfailing allegiance to serving the Eternal Reality that ought properly to inform and direct not only our comprehension of impermanent modes of reality, but also our grasp of the human and natural environment with its intrinsic logic of space/time events.

This early *Foreword* is written with such assurance and conviction as to suggest that the artist's visionary sensibility was his birthright and was not cumulatively acquired as a result of subsequent experience. The fact that all his writings give plentiful evidence of his struggle with an only partly com-prehending world should not blind us to this natal inheritance.

In one of the early Meditations Collins hints at the root need of the functionality of his art. 'I speak to the stillness in man, not to the activity'. (35) At once the habitual limits of human experience are opened up and expanded inwards. Art must serve the divine principle in man. In *Hymn of Life* the artist writes:

> For like attracts like. God, happiness, exist all the time in rays and
> vibrations that pour forth abundantly, eternally, what we have
> to do, and all we can do, is to magnetise our natures by purity of
> heart, so that we attract these rays and vibrations to us, for love
> attracts love, it is the Godlike in us that desires God. (54)

It is this principle that gives rise to the necessity to understand the nature and function of illusion, for there can be no assimilation of the Divine Reality where error and deception are present on the part of the knower. Only in the integral purity of our being can there be discernment of the Real from the unreal. The notion of illusion penetrates to the heart of Collins's creativity – the poetic, the didactic, as obviously the pictorial. How and where is the Real located and what are its directive implications so far as the artist is concerned? As Collins concluded early on,

> The Artist is he who is master of illusions,
> the non-artist is he who is subject to illusions. (42)

The theme runs on into Book Two of the Meditations: 'Art is the illusion by which we can understand Reality.' (48) and 'God is the Reality that makes the world an illusion.' (49)

It is difficult to determine to what extent this record of his mental outlook helped Collins to formulate the iconography of his art. Perhaps the writings were prompted in some way by his search for an objective, symbolic language to express his visual sensibility. But given the elegant discernment of the earlier writings it is possible to make the claim that his 'poetic' talent matured before his grasp of an objective, symbolic, pictorial language. To this day these Meditations have lost nothing of their pristine freshness of expression.

The 'mastery of illusion' is much more than a radical examination of personal experience. The 'vested interests of the ego' must certainly be challenged if the danger of mere solipsism is to be overcome. Though the mode may be subjective the nature of the inner God demands a type of purification that leads to an effective sacramental experience.

Collins started, as he confessed, with 'uneducated imagination' as a child. That is, uneducated in respect of the needs and rights of that mediation between inner and outer worlds that all imaginative images must possess. Over the years the painter came to understand how such images must have some grounding in the permanently Real. They cannot be left simply to the impulses and whims of an unrooted imagination. His writings are a record of his learning how the world of space and time is 'unreal' when seen in the light of the Eternal. For all its seeming 'solidity' from the perspective of sensory perception, it is from the viewpoint of the eternally present moment that is at the heart of personal witness that the world's fleeting, illusory nature is unveiled.

The artist's use of symbols must objectively arrest the flux of natural existence if it is to catch what underwrites it – the 'current of unified being' as he described it much later in our recorded conversation, published as *Theatre of the Soul* in 1979. The true symbol, far from being merely a reflected image in the sensorium, brings the seer, the thing seen and the act of seeing into that interpenetrating rapport that is the vital condition of unity of being where consciousness itself is absorbed into 'the Divine Reality reflected in the living wholeness of life as it is'. (170) Collins spoke with precision about this transfiguring moment of vision at the end of *Theatre of the Soul*. And in one of the *Selected Meditations* we find:

> All profound Truth is against Nature.
> Because an act is natural it does not justify it,
> because Nature shall be purged and wrought from the seeds and
> roots of Eternity. (133)

Collins was prepared to acknowledge that the Surrealists had, from a certain point of view, proved that the world is illusion. But what did not accompany the proof was 'the context of redemption', (141) as he repeatedly called it, that is logically demanded as a measure of the world's 'unreality'. In the surreal image nothing is transfigured, the world is merely rearranged. For Collins art is not an *escape* from 'the vanity and burden of external knowledge'. (149) True creativity is the management of illusion that reveals to the 'eye of the heart' the spiritual context the intellect demands, to distinguish the Real from the unreal. 'The act of creativity is an act of discernment into the nature of reality'. (126)

The all-important 'context of redemption' is an implied presence in everything that Collins did, and is perhaps the chief instance of where we must turn to the writing in order to gain entry to a dimension of his total vision that is not accessible from his visual art alone. For Collins the context of redemption is not only the pre-condition that validates the practice of art, it is also the very substance that nourishes the appreciation of true art.

The artist's writings show him coming gradually to a fuller understanding of the metaphysical implications of his visual and metaphysical dialectic. Only as late as the seventies did he become totally convinced, as he told me, that there was real substance to his 'dialectic' – that it made manifest something 'universal . . . going on in everybody'. (163) 'The substance of my art . . . is obviously being fed, there's food in it'. (167)

We must remember that most of these writings were unpublished and unknown during the artist's lifetime. The text for which he was best known, and which for most of his audience represented his singular declaration of artistic intent was his essay *The Vision of the Fool* of 1944. This was. however, preceded by 'The Anatomy of the Fool' (see p. 48 below). With the benefit of hindsight it is clear that these texts (in essence) say little that had not already been expressed in the earlier poetic Meditations. Indeed, the essay is really a summary collection of his earlier thoughts, but with added attention being paid to the figure of the Fool. This was to become his primary and orientating symbol from the early forties onwards.

We note the impassioned tone of most of the 1947 manifesto – a tone that was already present in the 1935 *Foreword*. Echoing Blake's exhortation in his Preface to *Milton* to the 'Young Men of the New Age' to rise up against the sterilities of the materialistic Enlightenment, Collins in turn calls for art to become the instrument for the realisation of the 'Eternal Person of all persons – God'. (103) This is hardly a call for the re-shuffling of the cultural *status quo*. It is a demand for the reinstatement of the contemplative life as the foundation of all artistic practice.

As the 'inviolate eternal innocence', the Fool is the guardian of 'the essential poetic integrity of life'.(99) His presence at the well-springs of life fixes the interior gaze of the soul by the clarity of his impartial vision. In the purity of his fully conscious life he deflects the spectator away from the abstractions generated by 'the vested interest of the ego', towards an absorption that concentrates and embodies a recognition of the 'supreme holiness of all human identity'. (101)

Given the complexity and depth of reference to the figure of the Fool in this essay (and elsewhere), we might well doubt whether Collins could have fully accounted for this theme by pictorial means alone. In the text the Fool is deployed as an instrument for a radical inversion of cultural values. But it is also evident that the artist was at the same time exploring his own responses to the implicit meanings of his central symbol. There can be no question that, both in the writings and in his pictorial representations of the Fool, the latter never simply illustrates the former. Collins's claim that 'the message is implicit in the nature of the medium', (92) as we will see, points us in the direction of appreciating the distinct qualities of the Fool, both as an image of iconic beauty as well as a directive idea with archetypal resonances. In his many pictorial manifestations, expressed through the idiom of colour, shape, line, rhythm and the nuances of mood these evoke, the Fool is a presence that renews our 'covenant made with the Divine Reality'. (148) As an object of mind, in the writings the Fool is a disposition to strip away the accretions of the rational mind, with its tendency to assert exclusive rights to the limits of our response to the wonder of created existence. In the writings, the Fool is a state of mind. In the pictorial images he is the witnessing presence of intuitive evocation. 'A man is granted as much life as he can imagine', (134) as the artist pointed out.

Another theme that only becomes fully explicable by recourse to Collins's writings is that of music. 'There are no objects in my paintings', (152) Collins insists. What, then, are we looking at when we see the Fool, the Angel, the Oracle, the child, the female Anima abroad in the imaginal space of their being?–a space that seems as much internal to them as external. Whether by their hieratic stasis or in their ritualized gestures and movement, wearing the garments of their contemplative vision–so often solitary; in the many heads whose gaze has the ambience of reverse perspective; in all these images we confront a world that challenges but does not destroy our expectations of the nature of representation. Here we are far from the observed, discrete object registered as a 'likeness' of something external, something 'other' than the observer. Here are the figures of possible states of being, their countenances turned towards us to solicit our assent to our spiritual birthright. If art is an effective component of the contemplative life then these images exist to aid the recovery of Paradise. To the extent that our true being is present before them, so we initiate the process of our own regeneration. By our contemplative presence we transmute the mystery of consciousness into a field of sacramental communion that belongs to all things. Truly absorbed in these 'non-objects', we discover their power to 'shift the accent from the events of consciousness to consciousness itself.' (109)

Here again we are guided by the writings in our understanding of the artist's intentions. Given the challenge of his radical approach to pictorial images as symbolic, transformative agents of states of consciousness, we more readily see why the artist speaks from the beginning about his art as the 'visual music of the kingdoms of the imagination'. (29)

That description comes from the early *Foreword*. In his subsequent writings (as well, of course, as in his pictorial works), Collins elaborated his understanding of the interchange of expressive possibilities between music and painting. In *Theatre of the Soul* he spoke of 'the whole feeling of flow and rhythm and texture and length of phrase, pulsating rhythm', (155) as characteristics of music that could be applied to his imagery. This is to invoke the gift of music to touch the soul without the aid of any confirmation from the outer world of objective experience. The ability of music to transcend the habitual perception of the physical offers the artist, by analogy, a befitting vocabulary with which to express the ineffable reality of permanence that sustains the transient, visible world. In our conversation Collins spoke of his paintings as being 'new musical chords' (162) that might be set to 'vibrate with one's sense of the divine'. (166) Needless to say, perhaps, such a transformation could not take place outside of the ambience of 'the aesthetic emotion of beauty'. (83) For Collins the transformative power of Beauty is feminine and generative in respect of the illusional powers of nature to clothe the invisibly Real. 'Poetry and beauty being attributes of God, they therefore can be a way to God'. (88)

In the first sentence of the *Foreword* we read 'the time has come when the people of the world, artists and poets in particular, should turn a sceptical eye upon the stereotyped actualities of the scientist and the politician'. (29) This is the artist setting out on his life-long intellectual preoccupation. It is a formidable challenge. So radical did it prove to be that he was, in effect, condemning himself (again, like Blake before him) to years of solitary under-appreciation within the cultural fraternity. It must have struck the reader so far that in virtually all of his pronouncements, Collins stood in opposition to more or less every intellectual and artistic axiom of the modernist agenda.

The artist was never in any doubt as to the root cause of the need for this opposition: an exclusively materialist, rational approach towards any understanding of what constitutes reality. Science, and its *modus operandi* (what he later came to call 'process knowledge'), is the generation of quantitative, statistical information extrapolating from which arises the technology that now shapes and conditions the human environment. Within this 'process' the soul is virtually eradicated, both as a means to cultural enlightenment, and as the integral organ of spiritual transformation. In the desacralised, mechanical universe bequeathed by modern science, it is the calling of the artist to remind us of our vocation for the eternal.

No amount of 'process knowledge' can be transmuted into 'why knowledge' in order to give the heart and the intellect that intimation of love and certainty for which they crave and for which they are created. Moreover, no amount of 'process knowledge' can provide the 'context of redemption' of the absolute and the eternal that is both logically and intuitively demanded by our experience of the mystery of consciousness. 'Why' knowledge is the context of 'how' knowledge, as Collins explained in *Art and Modern Man.* (1964) 'The language of "how" knowledge is concerned with communication of information; "Why" knowledge is . . . concerned with . . . communion and vision. This is why one of the basic languages of "why" knowledge is art and the symbol.' (109)

No art can possess meaning and significance in isolation from the presence of its witness. Its value is in its power to bring the soul fully to a consciousness of its own epiphany – the realization of its own freedom in the eternally supra-human. 'Art is a point of interpenetration between worlds, a marriage of the known with the unknown.' (112) It is the unknown that refreshes our lives, that 'virginity of consciousness' that refuses the exclusive imposition of worldly experience. In the child such virginity is a gift of Grace. For the adult there is always the awareness that such a gift comes from the far side of a consciousness of self. The child the Fool always remains is the embodiment of this refreshment.

To what extent was Collins's thought original? We have seen that it certainly goes to the origins of things, if we grant the notion of originality its fundamental meaning of 'coming from the source'. The idea that the artist is 'original' in virtue of some stylistic innovation is a presumption that has no place in the appreciation of Collins's work. In declaring that it has always been his intention to explore art as metaphysical experience, the artist consciously aligned himself with the values and meanings of the esoteric dimension of the various sacred traditions. This alignment proposes that art can act as an adjunct to the realization of the divine in the human. Both in his writings and in his symbolic imagery he is, in effect, proposing that the artist has to deal with the fundamental sources of Life: not art as the expression of private feelings; not art as the illustration of a personal viewpoint on the world; and certainly not art as an exclusively aesthetic occupation. For all these are, from Collins's standpoint, limited modes of consciousness addressed to specific areas of human experience. The spiritual revolution he demanded in the early *Foreword* was to be a return to the nature of consciousness itself, the one, eternal, original identity on which all human experience is predicated. The artist had surely taken to heart the teaching of the *Shvetashvatara Upanishad*: 'He is the One and only God, the self-luminous principle who is hidden in the heart of all beings. He pervades all and is the innermost essence of all beings. He governs all actions. He abides in all as the Witness. He is absolute consciousness and free from all qualities.'

What is the major characteristic of Collins's thought, given the evidence of his writings? It is the obvious and frequent agreement between the written record of his thought and the traditional wisdom of the Scriptures, saints, sages and mystical poets of all ages. This resemblance no doubt began in a native affinity of temperament. Over the passage of time the writings reveal him, as we have already noted, moving from a poetic to a more didactic mode of expression. In both modes he was discovering and confirming the necessary correspondences his visionary sensibility shared with the mystical legacy of the ageless wisdom.

What is most remarkable about these writings, and might be said to add to the store of that legacy? Again, like Blake, Collins warned of the prevailing darkness. He kept a steady gaze on the coming light but was under no illusion that the world was not yet ready for it. This was because, more importantly, he understood how and in what ways the insufficiency of that dark is measured by the light. We need not withhold an approval of these writings simply because the artist did, from time to time, confess that he was not comfortable with words and was even suspicious of any verbal formulation of the act of creativity. By their beauty and profundity his writings will stand comparison with those of any British artist.

The writings embody a trenchant and profound critique of the modern age, questioning, as we have seen, its basic intellectual and cultural presumptions. Collins saw through the many shibboleths espoused in the name of 'art for art's sake' which have, with a gathering inevitability, impoverished the spiritual value of art over several centuries. In doing so, he held to the hope and inspiration of that Truth which is inscribed as the very substance of Being itself.

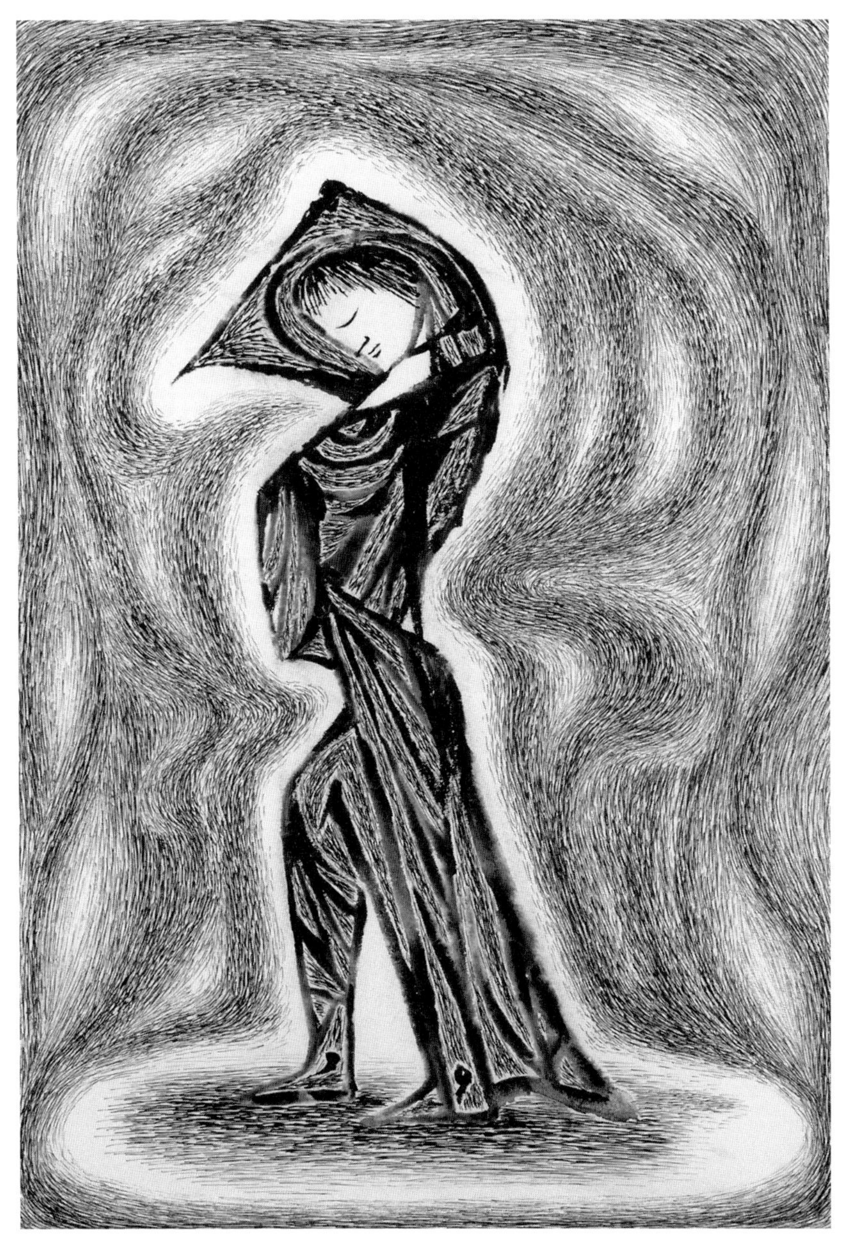

Hamlet 1959

(see plate 19)

The Artist as Image Maker

Because we fell from Paradise, Paradise exists. (46)

'The message is implicit in the nature of the medium'. (92) The painted or drawn image is, then, not simply a representation of what might equally well be expressed in words. The very substance with which the picture is made holds something of the significance of the image as a re-cognised state of being. In contrast to the purely abstract picture, here the painted image is more than the sum of its parts – pigments, graphite, and the like. The dimension of meaning is locked into the physical substance through which the image exists; a meaning none the less that is more than the medium of its expression. This seems paradoxical. It is certainly a distinction that needs careful handling in our time, since we must move beyond the specifically modernist aesthetic for which pictorial values are self-referential. As David Jones once pointed out, the value of art may be 'abstract', but that does not mean the abstract is art.

We need a defining line of approach in looking at Cecil Collins's images, one that releases the eye and the mind from the atrophied habits of modernism – an approach equal to the summons made by the images themselves. In this respect it is useful and illuminating to consider Collins alongside Jones, his friend and contemporary. These are the two 'outsiders' of modern British painting and the juxtaposition will help to identify Collins's distinctive understanding of the value and meaning of pictorial imagery.

Collins and Jones are positioned in relation to one another as two complementary faces of a single focal point that takes in the perspective of both the temporal and the timeless. The substance of Jones's art is freighted with the history of European Christendom, as it is ordered and transformed according to the trans-historical significance of the Catholic Mass. With Collins, on the other hand, the substance of his imaginative vision is that of the soul's participation in substantial existence, with the ever-present possibility of its illumination by the Divine – its primordial substance. From their shared focal point, Jones faces outwards and backwards, Collins inwards and forwards. Jones's images are taken from the cultural insignia of Christendom and observed reality. The presiding paradigm of his art is that of the artist as maker who works in the likeness of God as the Maker of all things. In these images the Divine is approached, as from afar, through the agency and power of human creativity to transfigure matter.

Collins's images possess no historical context at all and owe much less to the exact appearance of observed reality. They are iconic in the true sense of being the bearers of a divine presence. Collins's images are, therefore, instruments of self-transcendence. For this artist the image is an interior analogue which seeks to orientate and move the viewer's consciousness inwards to the realisation of its perhaps, as yet, unawakened possibilities, The presiding paradigm is that of the human soul pre-possessed by the Divine. David Jones's imaginative disposition envisages, for the most part, the outer world as charged with traces of Divine transcendence, while Cecil Collins's inclines to invoking the inner world of the soul as the theatre of enactment of the Divine immanence.

There is another important way in which the juxtaposing of these two artists may prove illuminating. It is integral to the art of both that their distinctive visions are realised against the implied background of the sense of loss and alienation that is a shaping characteristic of the spiritual crisis of the modern age. For Jones the 'sign of the times' that marks our spiritual regression is the loss of a sense of place and identity within the history and 'mythos' of our Christian cultural inheritance. In the late pictures especially, Jones collects and concentrates the cultural references of Roman and Christian and Arthurian symbols in order to arrest the loss of memory and the sense of uprootedness from a spiritual context such as precipitates the collapse of a cultural order. These late works are a resumé, a gathering together in an act of witness and celebration of what in the past man has embodied in his utile artefacts: those things he finds it increasingly difficult to *be* and do as a means of sanctification; modes of cultural action and spiritual assimilation no longer common among men.

For Collins, this same crisis is one of loss and alienation from Paradise.

Jones's symbols are anchored in the hope that they might yet stave off the coming abomination by reference to the trans-historical content of their meaning. Collins, on the other hand, sees only exhaustion, a dying externality in these canonic references – a metaphysical depletion of their transformative power faced with the downward 'drag' of historical degeneration. In looking to the light of a coming dawn Collins's images express the need for purification in the face of worldly decay and impoverishment. In this last respect these artists share a common goal: to make a stand against both the external and the internal negative forces that threaten to engulf us. Where Jones attempts to evoke a cultural pattern in historically collapsed and overlapping symbols, Collins invokes a lyrical consciousness that makes use of a simpler, more direct means of pictorial expression. Here, there are frequently no more than one or two figures against a background of primordial simplicity – often no more than a single head. The historical dynamic of Jones's imagery is complemented in Collins's work by a static gradation of mood that seeks to contain a given state of being. This inward movement of concentration carries with it a metaphysical obligation. As we have seen, Collins has left an eloquent written testimony of his understanding of what is demanded here.

> The artist is concerned to personify experience, to reveal the identity, the nuance, the being of things, the presence. He is interested in transforming the thing in the spontaneous creative moment, the unexpected moment of eternity, the moment of freedom; unexpected, because the unexpected moment is the unpossessed moment. This is perhaps one of the deepest insights of the creative experience; whereas in process knowledge intellectual possession is the essential condition prior to analysis. Therefore art is a kind of redemption of consciousness and environment. (108)

Collins's vision of the need for this healing redemption makes him *the* artist of the twentieth century who truly divines the diminishing current of life at the end of the historical cycle that is the modern age. These are the 'latter times' for which a certain metaphysical depreciation is the destined mark.

When, as now, negative impulses seem to prevail over positive, there are compensating possibilities of renewal at work in the deepest intuitions of imaginative consciousness. In their looking forwards–not assuredly to a passage through time, but to the expectation of the soul's recovery of its native element–Collins's images bathe us in the authentic springs of transformation.

His Fools, Sybils and Angels resonate with the presence of what is inviolate at the roots of consciousness. These figures are auguries of that joy and innocence that are prior to those worldly preoccupations that soil and tire us, casting their lengthening shadows of inadequacy upon every form of worldly accomplishment and distraction. To be amply present before such images is to be called to witness the incommensurabilty of worldly process with our full being. The proper condition of man's existence has always been and remains that of relating to essence–which is, ultimately, a question of self-identity. Collins's figures serve this inward act of identity by withdrawing the responsive viewer from an exclusive concern with worldly objects and sensations.

Cecil Collins's art is supremely the art of the imaginative, symbolic image. In his rejection both of abstraction on the one hand and of naturalism on the other, the artist acknowledges the abiding and intimate connectedness of form and mind. If the aspiration towards the spiritual (as distinct from the simply immaterial) through images, acting as the support for contemplation, is to be effective, then it follows that the image must have substance; must have a content. It is the appearance of something not wholly made present by external appearances. Look at the two vases of flowers. (plates 7 and 8) These are perfectly recognizable depictions of familiar things, but there is more, for these images owe a debt to two worlds; that of natural appearances as well as that of their unseen origins in the process of life itself. Perhaps in an unconscious echo of Palmer's early trees that are not quite recognizable botanical specimens, Collins's flowers are made to revel in the exuberance of their growth. His flowers grow out of pots that resemble a chalice – with all its incarnational resonances, here and elsewhere–the table top and cloth an altar, the pot itself patterned to suggest the flowing vitality of the life-force possessed by the waters hidden within it. The underlying context of such pictures is clearly the sacramental. If it is to have cognitive value the image must affirm something other than itself. In this sacramental context the image, to the extent that it engages our being, is a summons to inner action.

Indeed, the painter often referred to his art as being a 'Theatre of the Soul', 'not a place but a condition where the life of the soul is re-enacted'. (148) And so we find in many of the pictures a visual 'play' on this *condition* of re-enactment using the furnishings of theatrical production. Often the sides (occasionally the top also) of the picture form a pair of stage curtains drawn back to exhibit the scene, as in *The Artist and His Wife*, 1948 (plate 11) and, again, the *Vase of Flowers* (plate 8), where inner and outer worlds are conjoined. In such pictures the spectator looks out to a larger world, but in *The Man with the Lamp*, 1943 (plate 5) – an instance of many – the curtains and the stage boards are so placed as to include the spectator as part of the 'performance'. This arrangement of the curtain gives to it the connotation of revealing the soul's drama, as it were, externally. Often a single part curtain, part veil, drawn back, is placed in the middle distance as an emblem of the unveiling properties of the soul's internal enactment. (V. plates, 26, 27 and 32)

Along with the idea that the sole obligation of artistic images is to elicit a merely aesthetic response in the viewer goes the inference that art is cut off from the seamless matrix of living interconnectedness of values that gives life its meaning. So their claim upon us is weakened to the point where, ultimately, they negate the very condition of their validity. It is to suggest that it is not the very *raison d'être* of perception to engage intelligence, memory and imagination. The artistic image cannot possess any sort of quasi-absolute autonomy, but must carry a burden of meaning, and must, in consequence, by its nature, as we have seen, stand in some relationship to a discernment of what is real and what is unreal; it must stand in some relationship with truth. Such a relationship clearly raises the question of the ontological status of imagination.

At its simplest, imagination is the image-making faculty of the mind. An image in the imagination re-presents a likeness of an appearance. What we need to know is whether the likeness leads the mind away from the Real or towards it. If this option were not a property of the imaginative image, then either deception would not be possible or all images would be totally deceptive. Then, paradoxically, all such images would possess absolute veracity: the snake a coiled rope is mistaken for would be equally as real as the actual rope itself.

Even as they reject empirical observation as the arbiter of pictorial truth, as the language of imaginative discourse, Collins's archetypal images assent to appearances in so far as these envisage the unmanifest according to the normal modes of visual perception. We see this in *Hymn* (plate 6), for instance, where it is as if we are looking out of the window of our existential being on to an as yet uninhabited primordial scene, the picture surface itself a pane of transparency, being the invisible division that permits the interrelation-ship between two worlds. Looking beyond we see the repeated pulses of the rhythmic energies of the theophanic scene forming the likenesses of sea, clouds, an island of trees and in the distance, illuminating all, the flaming glory of the rising sun. We are here called upon to absorb these rhythmic energies.

The world of natural appearances is at all times the inviolable sanctuary from which these images grow and remain re-cognizable. Figures do not walk on the sky, trees do not grow from clouds, there is always a simulation of per-spective in the landscapes. The many heads all have recognizably 'human' faces, their many inner dispositions – revealed in their impassive gaze – modes of contemplation we might occupy, even when they seem, at times, to consist only of a few gestural strokes of pigment or graphite on the picture surface. They exist to enhance and vivify our apprehension of those spiritual energies that are the life-informing properties of the unknown. 'The reality of life is incomprehensible. Therefore the Poet and Artist creates an incomprehensible image of life'. (88)

'Painting is a metaphysical activity.' Nor is this to be understood as meaning that painting is an attempt to indulge the creative process as if it were a quasi-metaphysical experience. At its most mature and articulate, when it is informed by his most profound insight, Collins's imaginative language emerges from and surmounts the creative process to exist objectively. It has a dialectic. It is the instrument of a level of experience that is communicable in terms that relate to the knowledge and wisdom of the saint and the mystic. There are those who admire most the energy and the brilliance of his 'matrix' paintings, and it is through such works that his art is most likely to seem assimilable to modernist presuppositions. Nevertheless, Collins's mastery is undoubtedly at its quintessentially characteristic in the fully realized formal perfection of the iconic image. This is his unique contribution to the art of his time and will most likely confirm the measure of his significance beyond it.

'Painting is a metaphysical activity' since each work is a 'place' where the life of the soul is present, each 'place' being a momentary pre-figuration of the hidden unity of life. Such places cannot be 'located' since we only *see* them in a moment of initiation in that imaginative space where we are already pro-jected beyond the confines of our fragmentary, habitual world. In the utter serenity of the pencil drawing *Paradise* (1976; V. plate 44), for instance, we are absorbed and initiated into the pre-conscious mystery of our origin. Here is the palpable recreation of the gift of plenitude that is our first state of being. Such imaginative moments must be lived on the plane at which they are realized – that is, 'where' they *are*. An Angel's sensuous beauty, the clothing of its presence in painterly attire, parades before us an intimation of what, having fallen from it, we are called to return to. It is the 'space' of the Angel that we must inhabit. Angel, Fool, Sibyl, Anima, each by its presence utters some pulsation of that hidden reality.

This is why the artist makes his most audacious claim, 'there are no objects in my paintings', so that, as we noted when examining his writings, we should not attempt to correlate the content of his pictures in any literal way with the created world that comprises an indefinite number of discrete entities, the world of opposites and differentia where one thing is seen and known never to be another. The world inhabited by Collins's figures is never conditioned by this law of discrete existence. Here we have to reverse the habits of outward perception to recognise that one thing has the possibility to become another by way of their common, pre-fallen source. Collins's scenery is the soul's impalpable habitat, its occupants its figurative guises. All these figures and scenes are the implements of a gnosis of association and relationship of the impalpable connectedness of things. Thus in many of the works, what appears to be a structural device, the visual rhyme, has a further significance: the texture of a tree trunk is also that of a river, hair is like water, the foliage of a tree is the shape of a wing, an angel's wing is that of a butterfly or is a leaf, grasses are flames or waves of the sea, tree trunks shoot up like volcanoes to burst into cloud-like foliage, scattered flowers, we realize, but fallen stars. A fool holds a butterfly that returns his gaze as from a 'human' face – a moment emblematic of the friendliness of all living things. We have already recorded Collins's account of the initiatory moment of the bird in a tree (see *V*. p. 57) which led him to find a pictorial analogy for the intuition of the primordial unity.

As we have also seen, Collins rejected the 'puritanism' (as he called it) of abstraction because it posits a world of mental forms torn away from the inclusive and indivisible, abiding unity of life. The eloquence of this unity is, for this artist, no less present in an insect's wing, a bird, a mountain as they are contemplated in the soul, than in the spectrum of colours refracted into the modes of poetic consciousness. Because 'imagination is the organ of the interior nature' the artist discovers in these modes of poetic consciousness, as they are realized in the particularity of their image, the beauty that is proper to the human. As Plotinus states in the Fifth *Ennead*: 'We ourselves possess beauty when we are true to our own being; our ugliness is in going over to another order; knowing ourselves, we are beautiful, in self-ignorance we are ugly.'

With Collins's artistic language we must accustom our eyes to a world whose expression bears little or no resemblance to that of any other artist. To be sure he did not 'invent' the Angel, any more than the Eternal Bride. But at his touch they are unerringly of his vision. To play the game of source hunting is already to defer to a slack, unfocused perception. Such is the nature of the iconic image that it demands all our attention or nothing, not as an idolatrous object, but because it discloses its inviolate substance only to our utmost response. That is part of the challenge and the rebuke of these images. In the totality of our absorption there must be no interval to be occupied by familiar

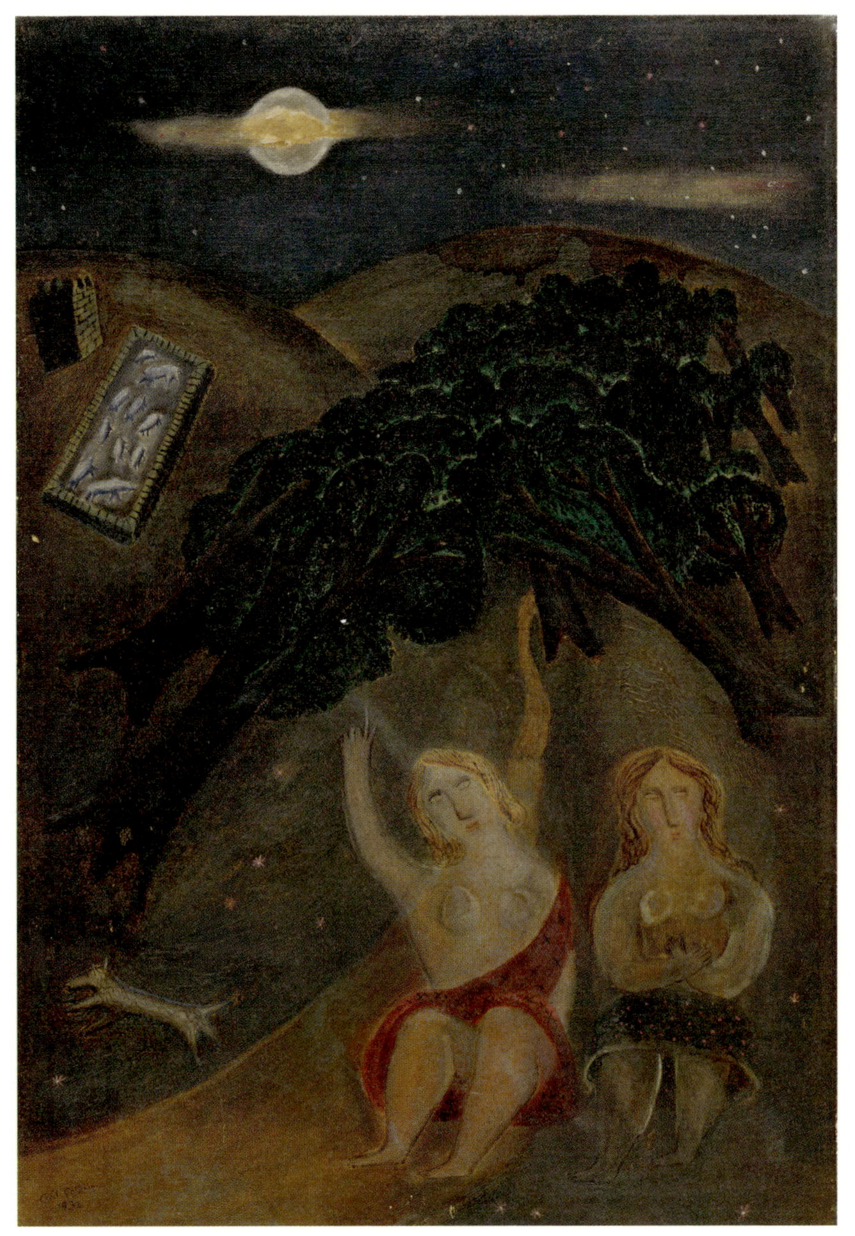

1 Night 1932
oil on canvas, 76.2 × 51

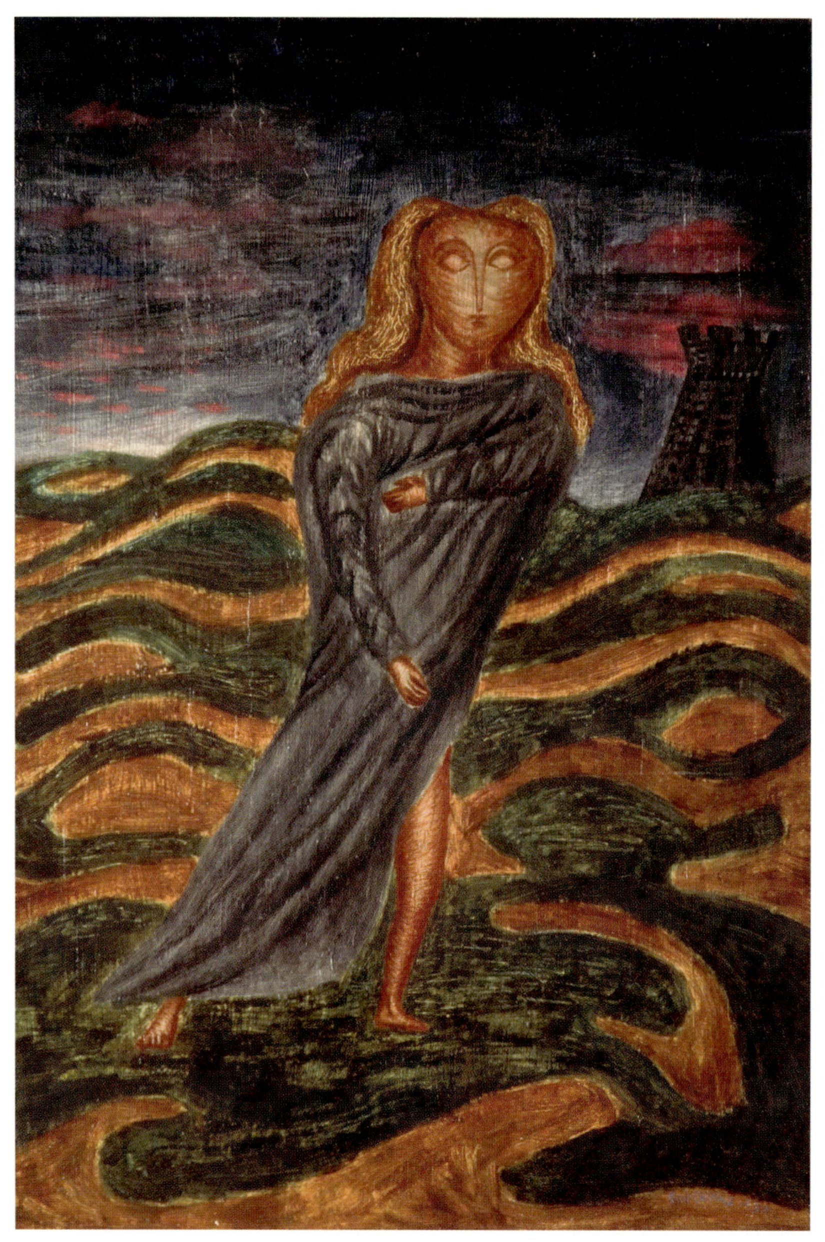

2 *The Pilgrim* 1934
oil on canvas, 40.5 × 30.5

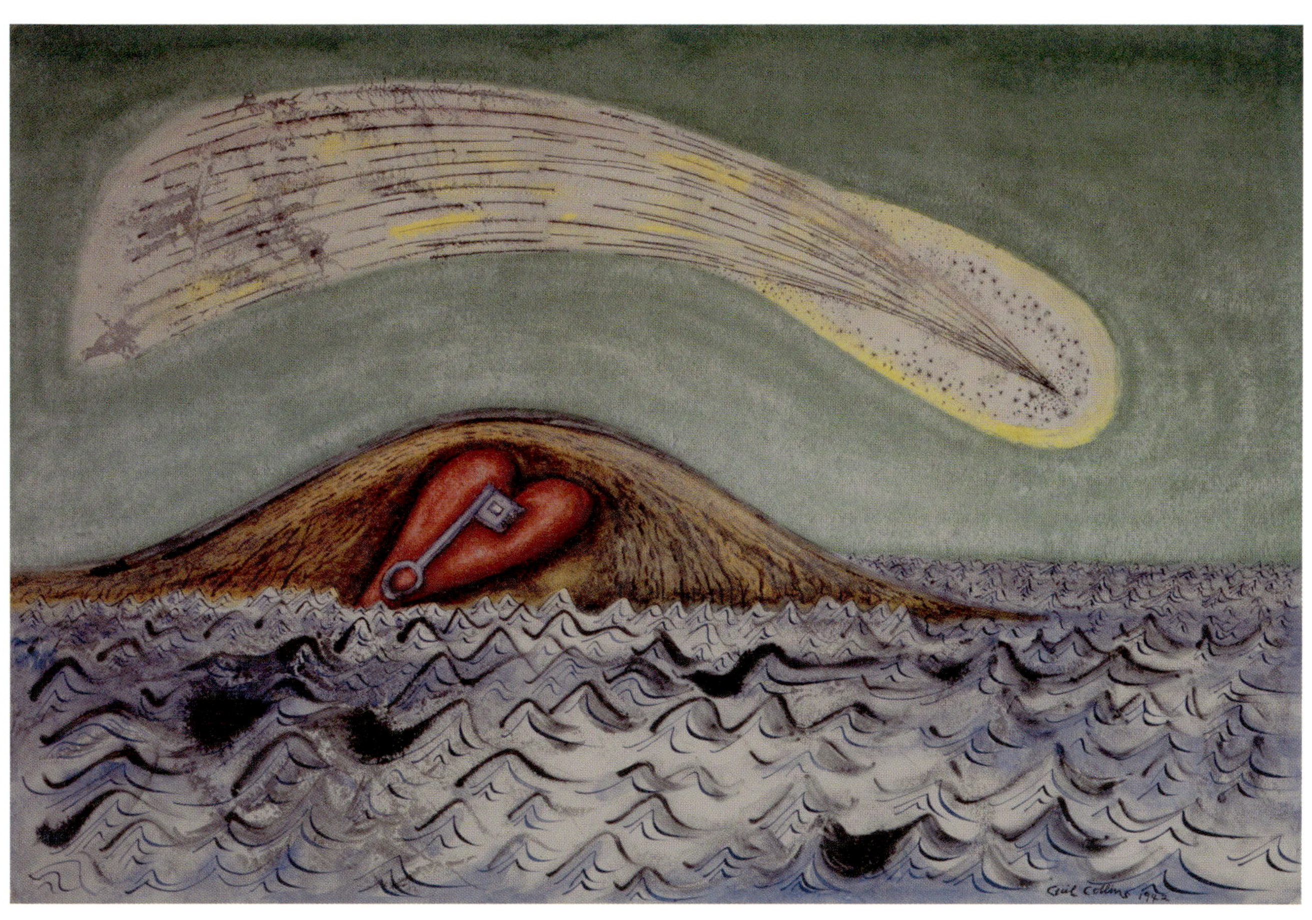

3 *Thy Thoughts O Life* 1942
watercolour and ink on paper, 38 × 56

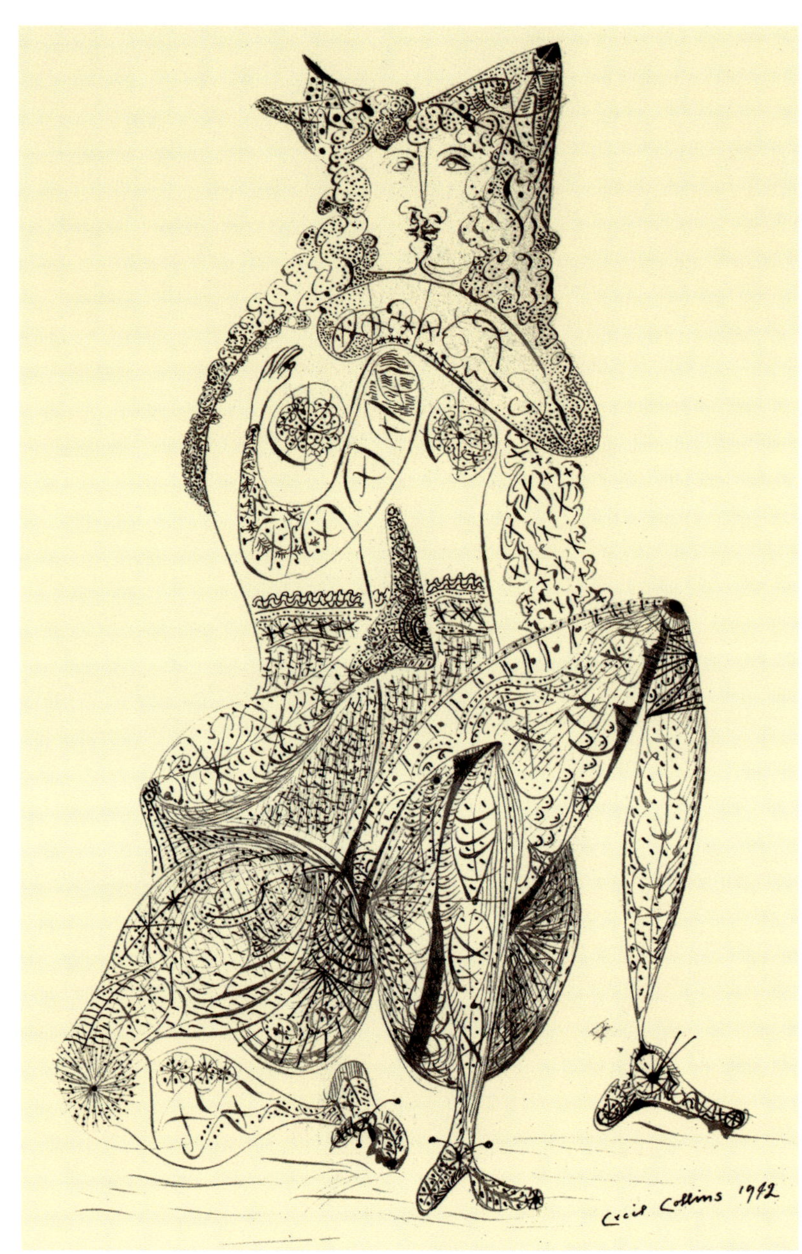

4 [Fools Embracing] 1942
ink on paper

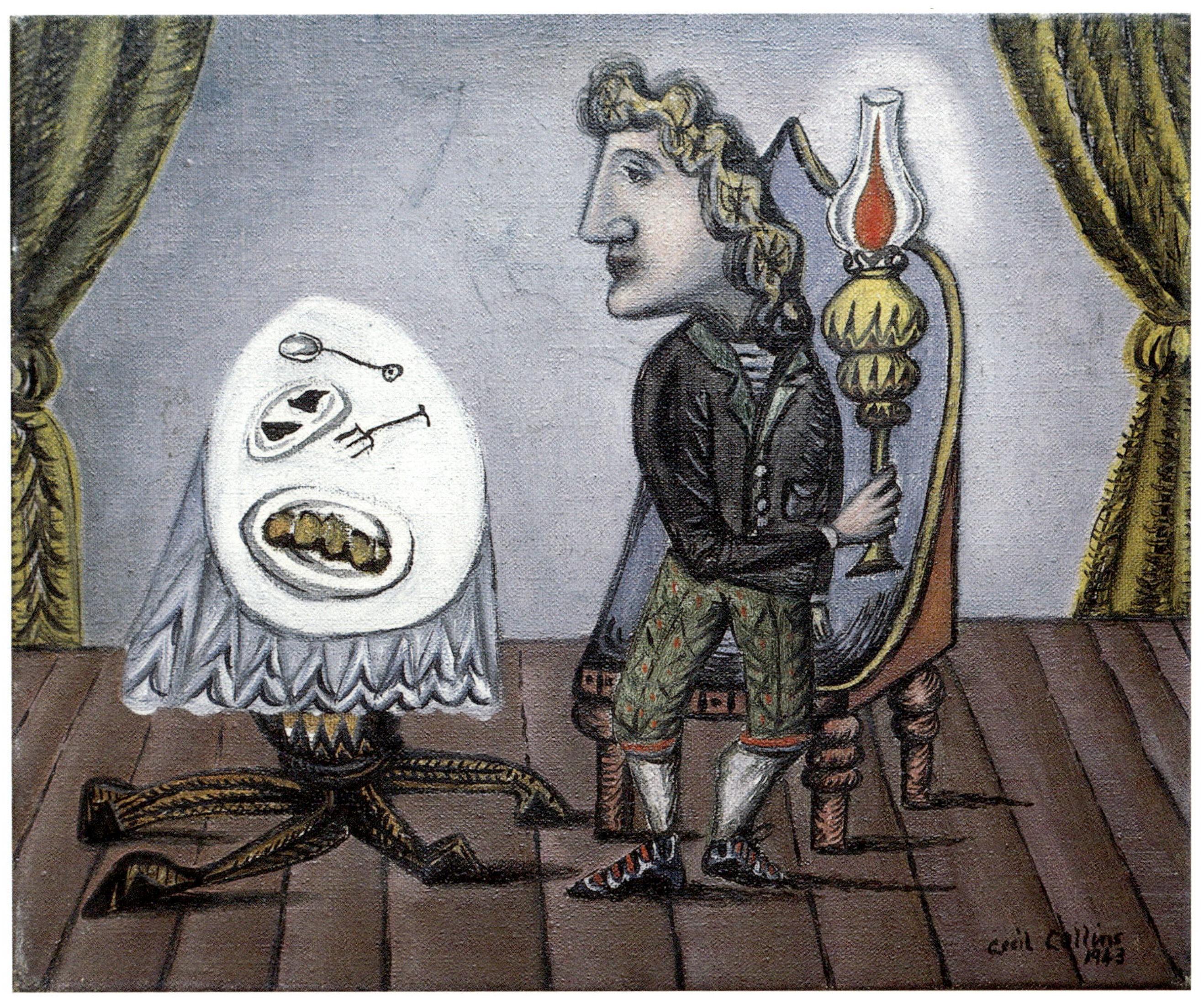

5   The Man with the Lamp   1943
oil on canvas, 25.4 × 30.6

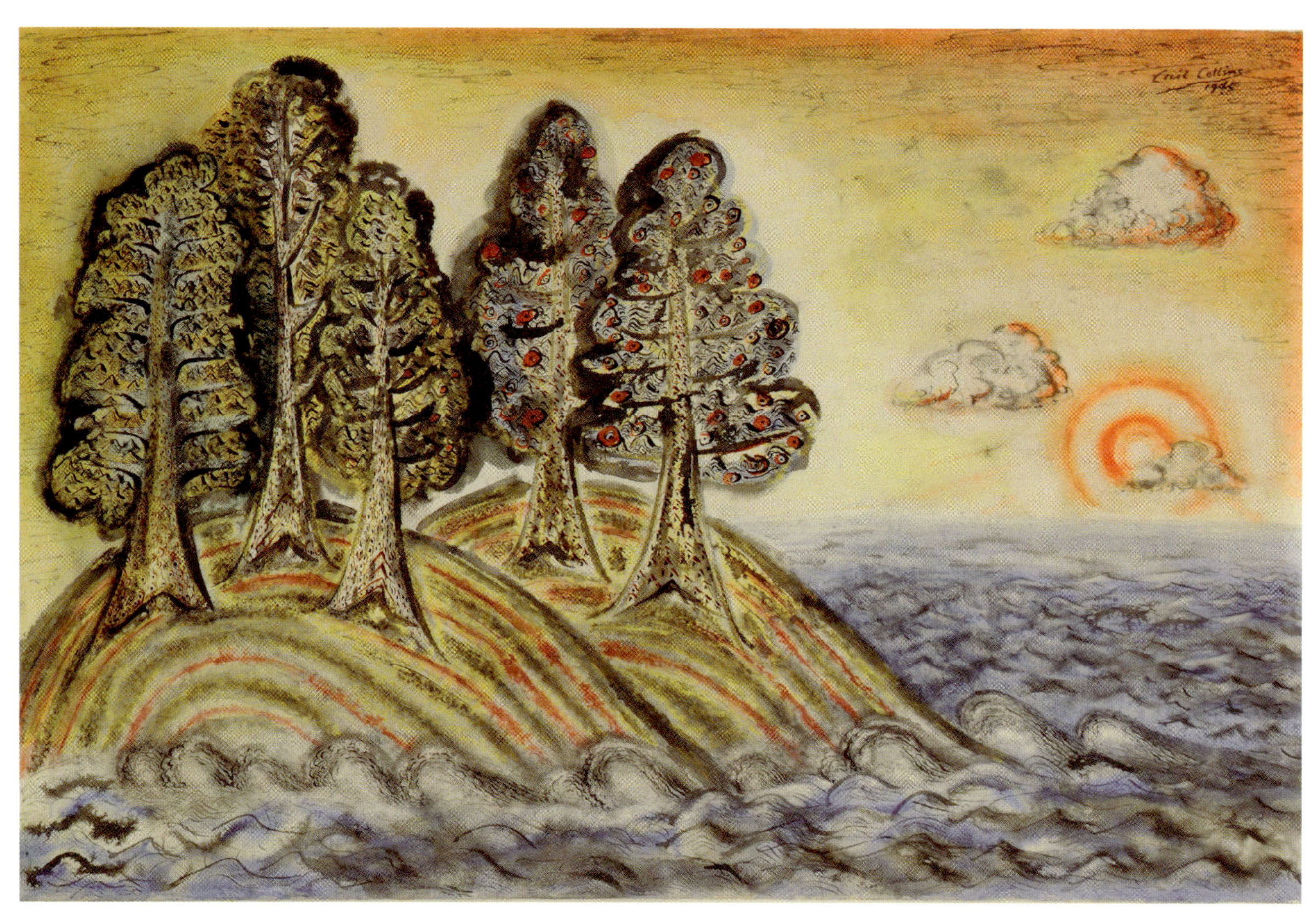

6 *Hymn* 1945
watercolour and pastel on paper, 32.5 × 55.9

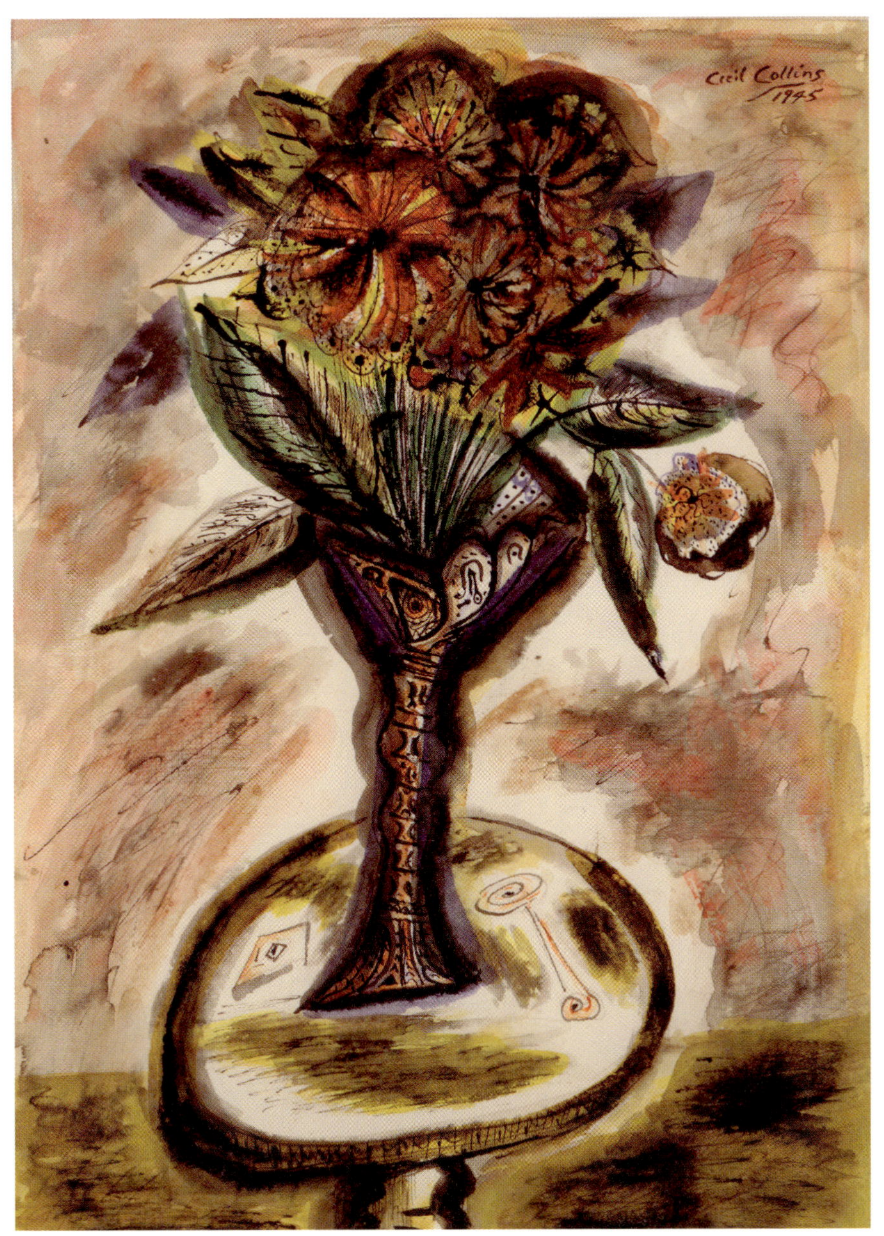

7 *Vase of Flowers* 1945
watercolour and ink on paper, 32.5 × 25.5

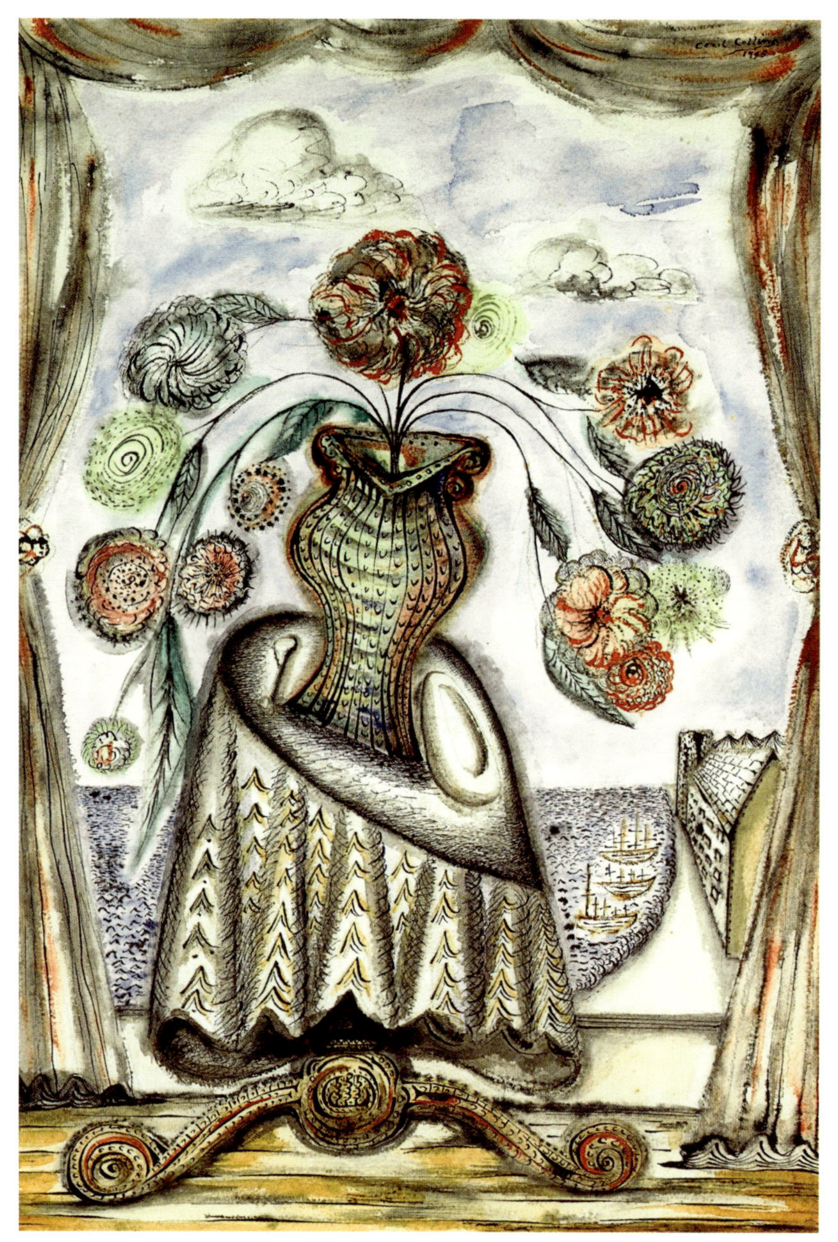

8 Still Life 1945
watercolour, 62 × 43

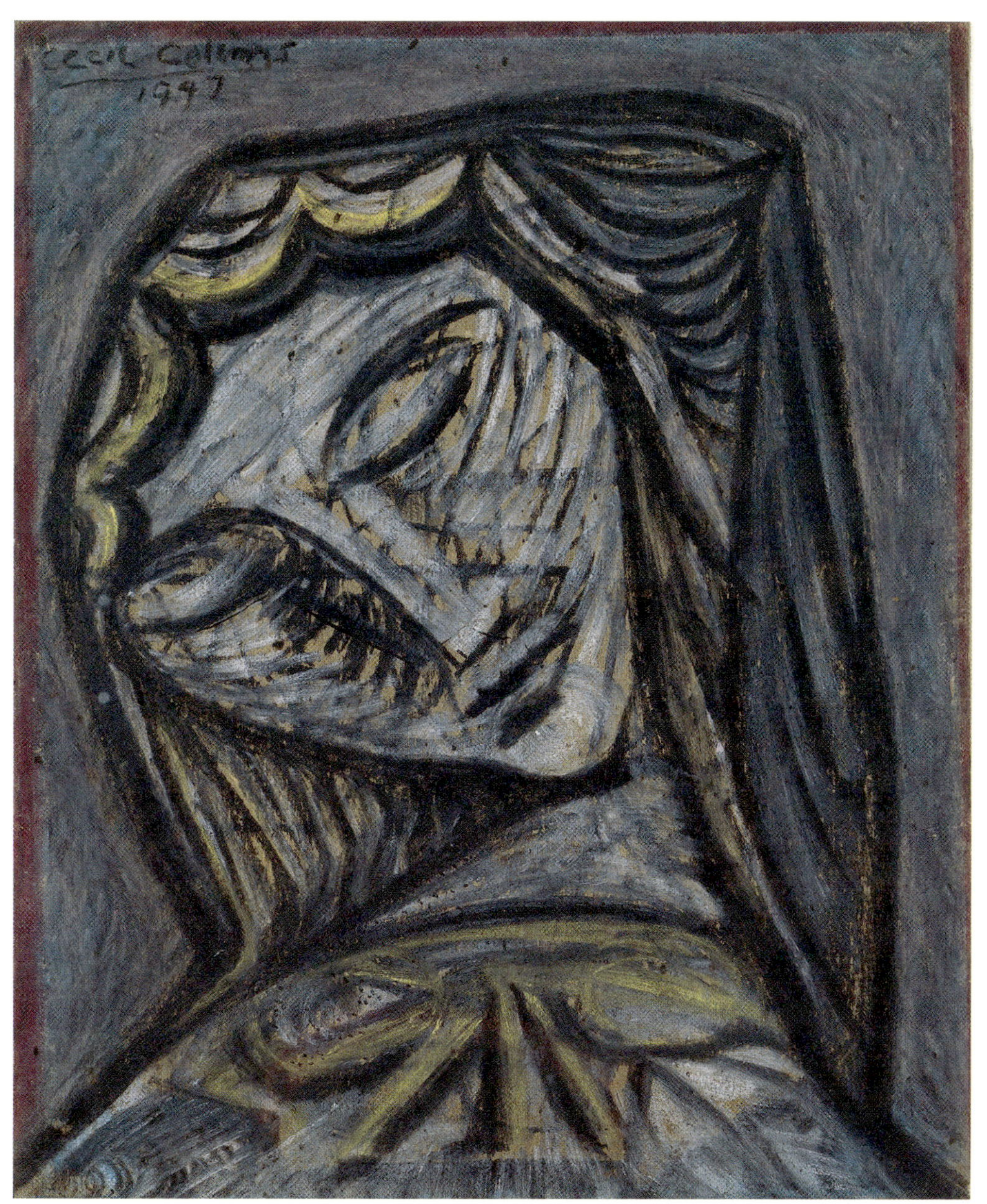

9 Head 1947
pastal on paper, 24 × 19

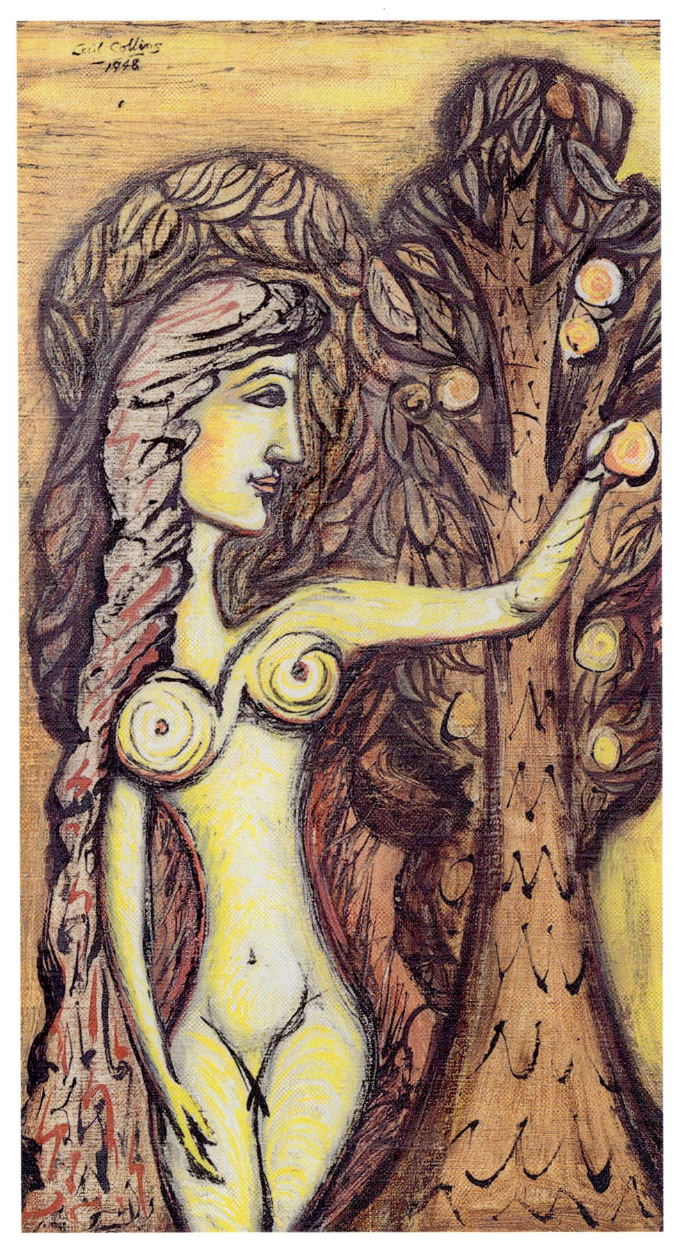

10 Eve 1948
oil on canvas, 45 × 23

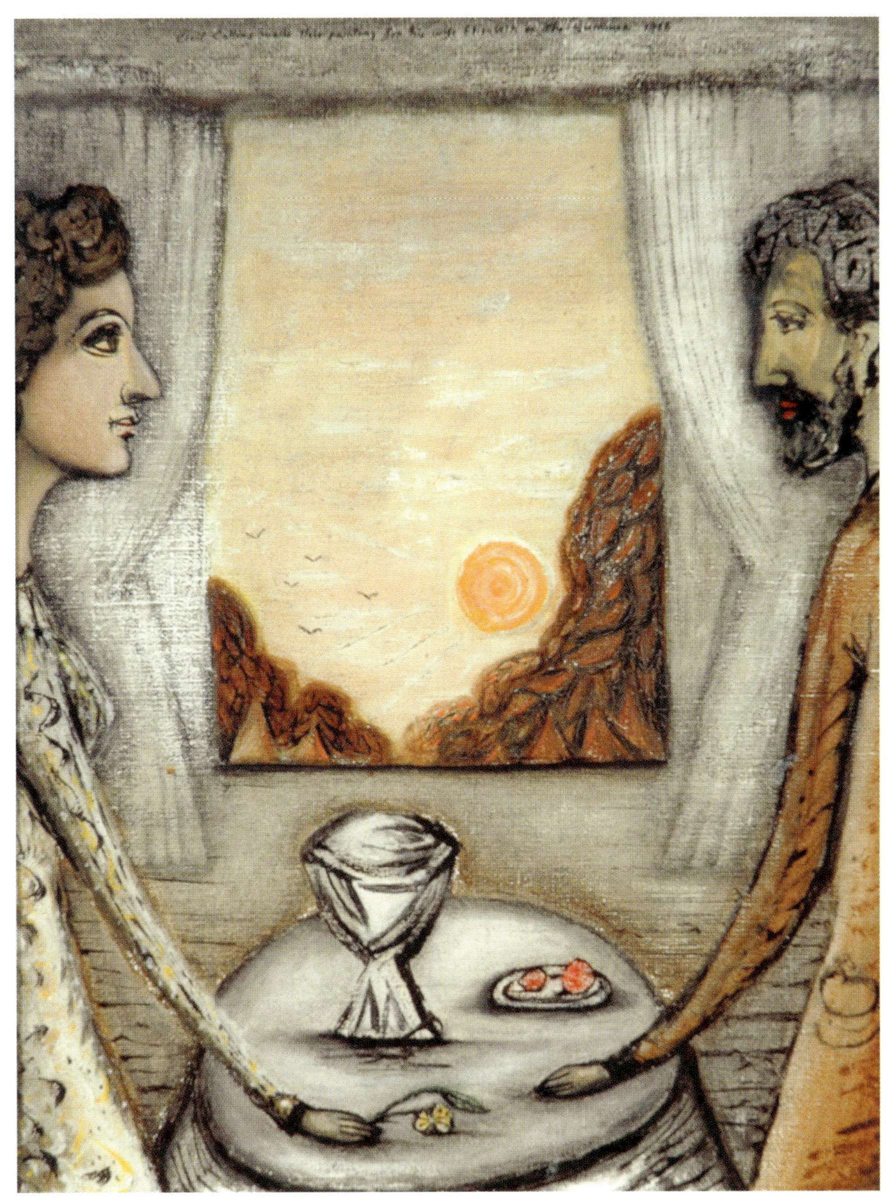

11   *The Artist and His Wife*   1948
oil on canvas, 40.5 × 30
(Inscribed 'Cecil Collins made this painting for his wife Elisabeth in the Summer of 1948')

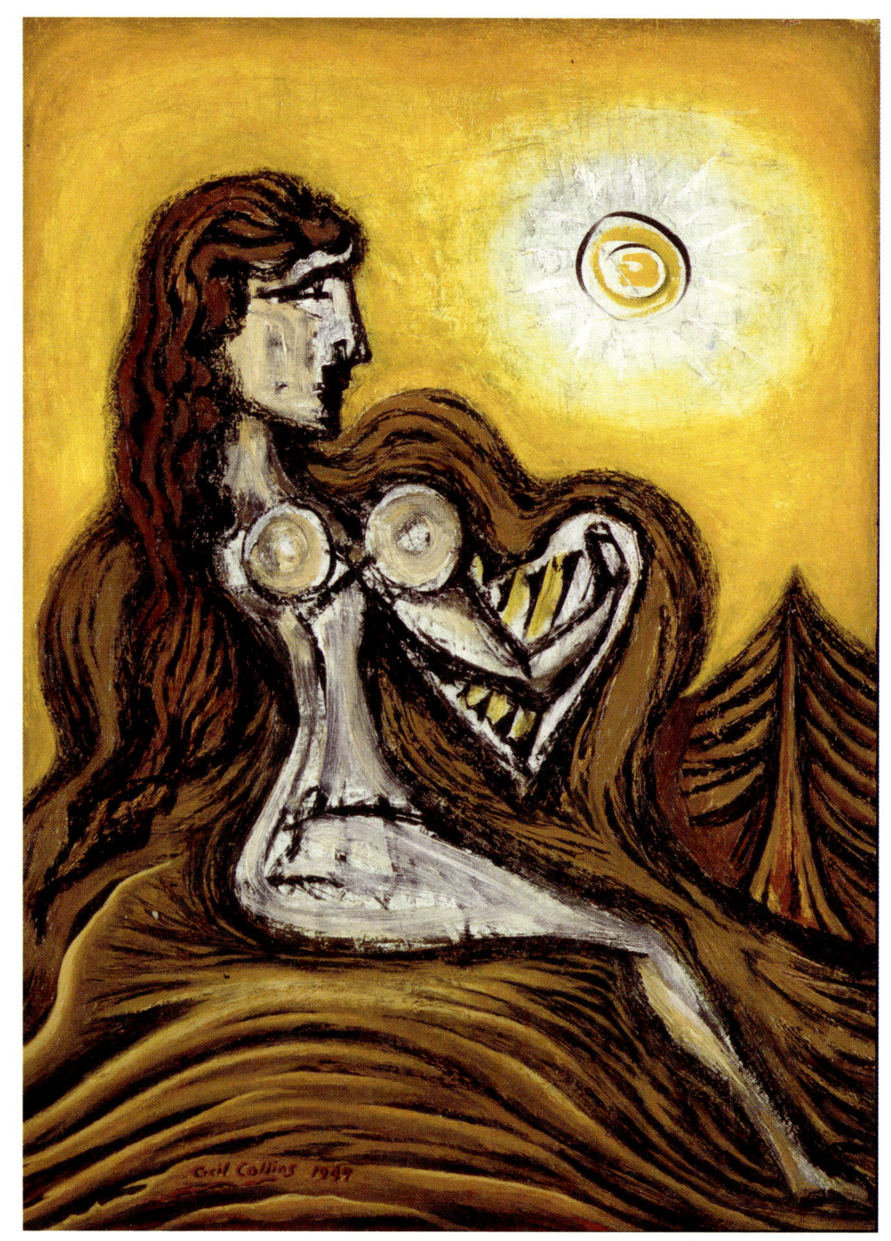

12 Pastoral 1949
oil on canvas, 35.5 × 25.5

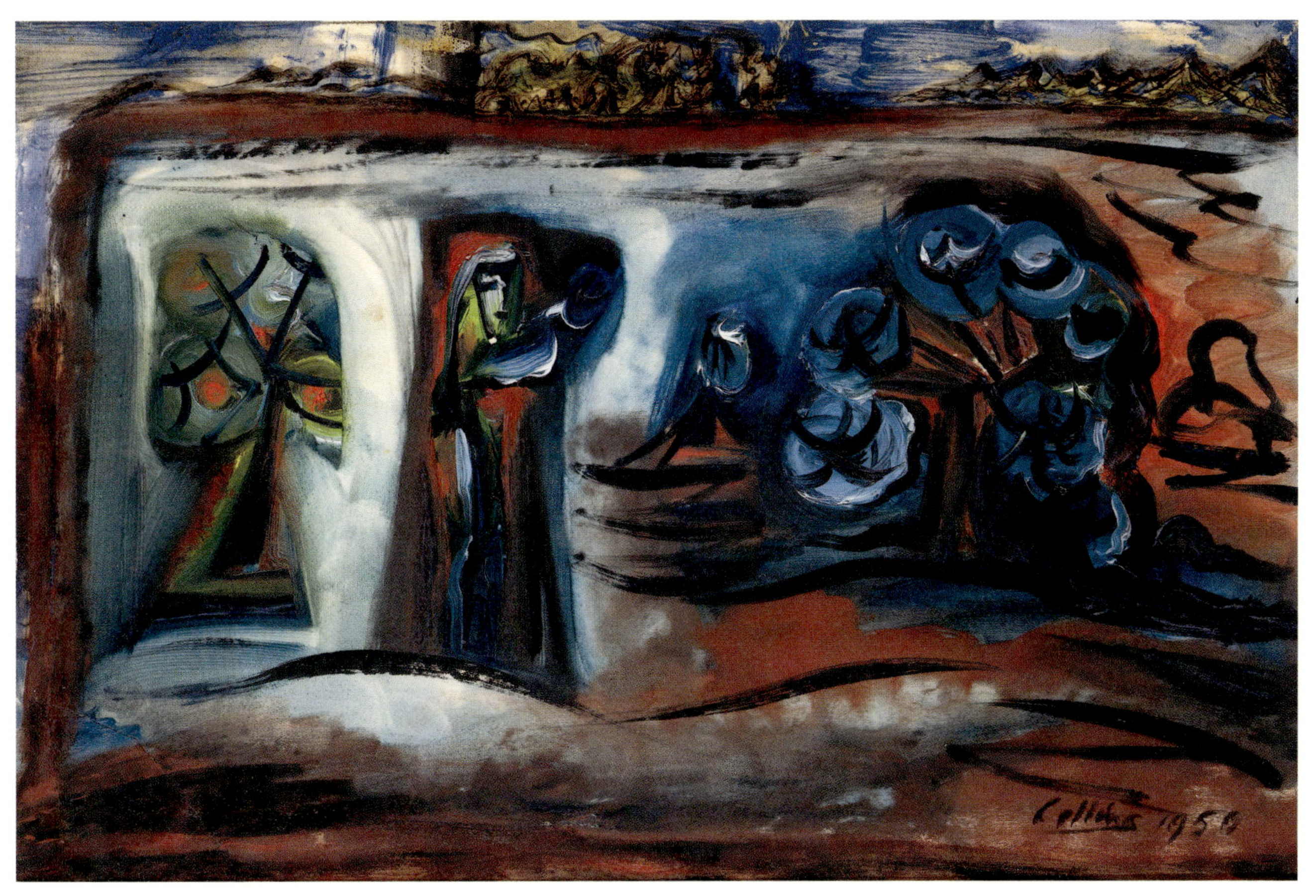

13 Pastoral 1950
oil on paper laid on card, 23.5 × 37.5

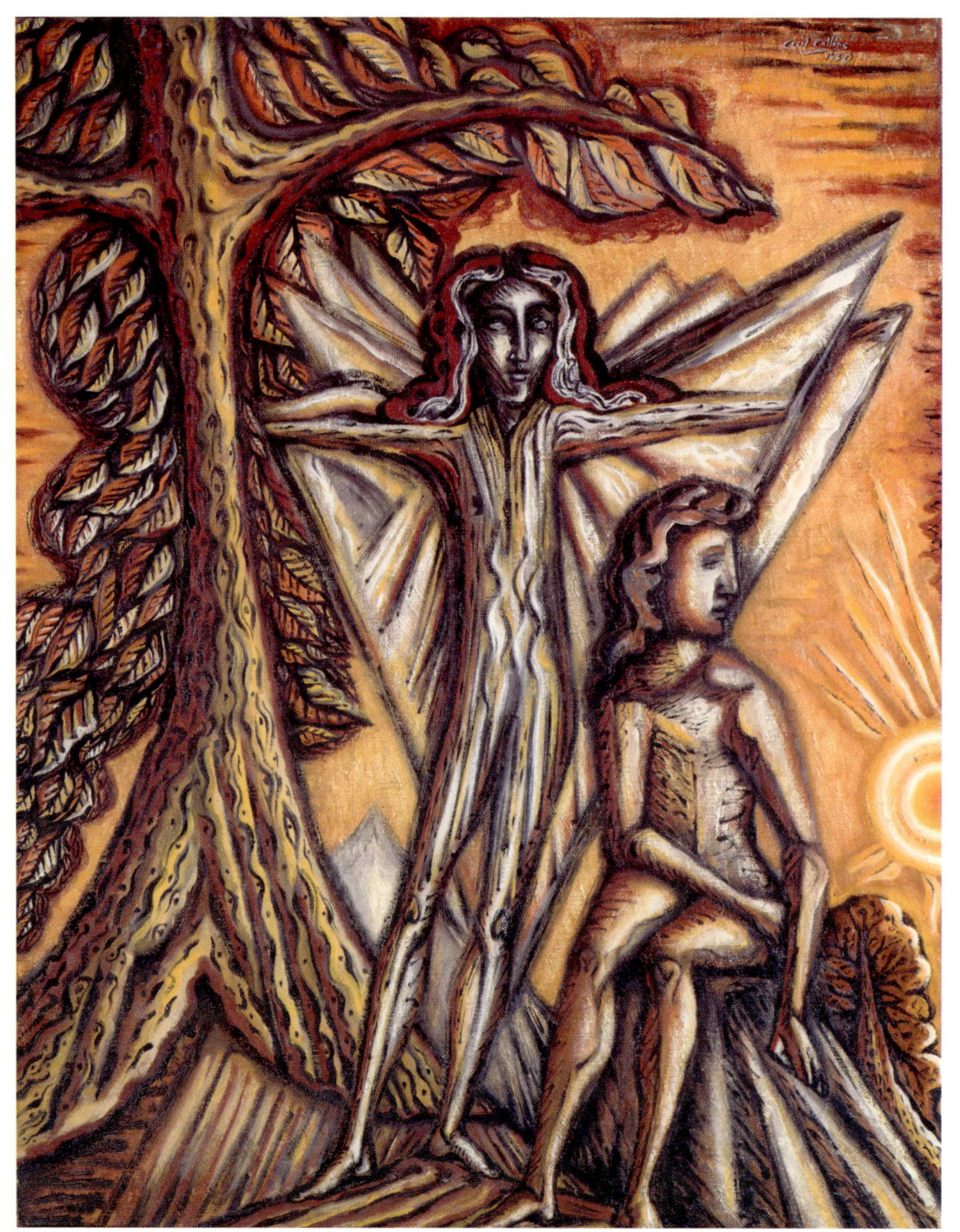

14 *Angel with Adam* 1950
oil on canvas, 81.3 × 61

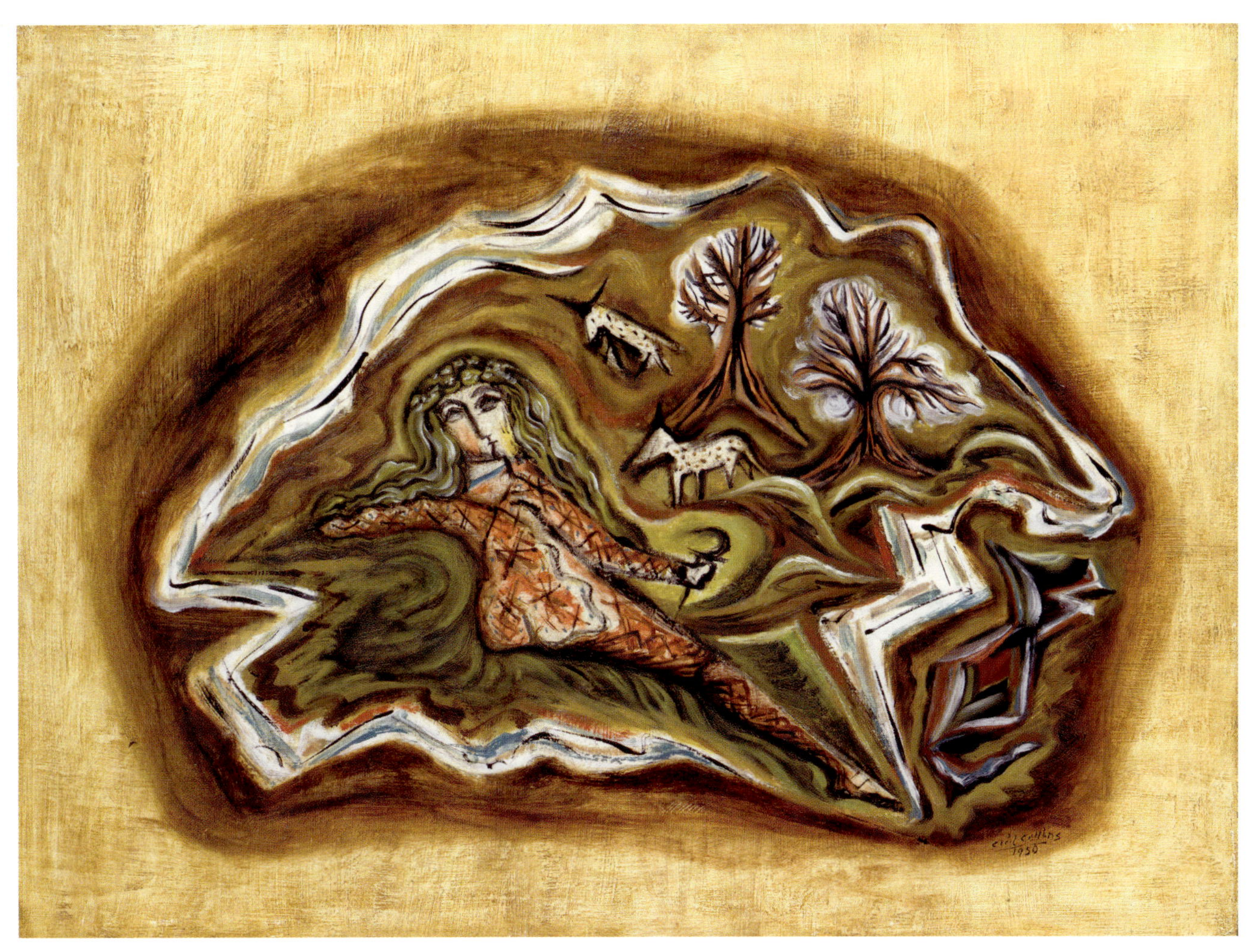

15 Pastoral 1950
oil on board, 44 × 59

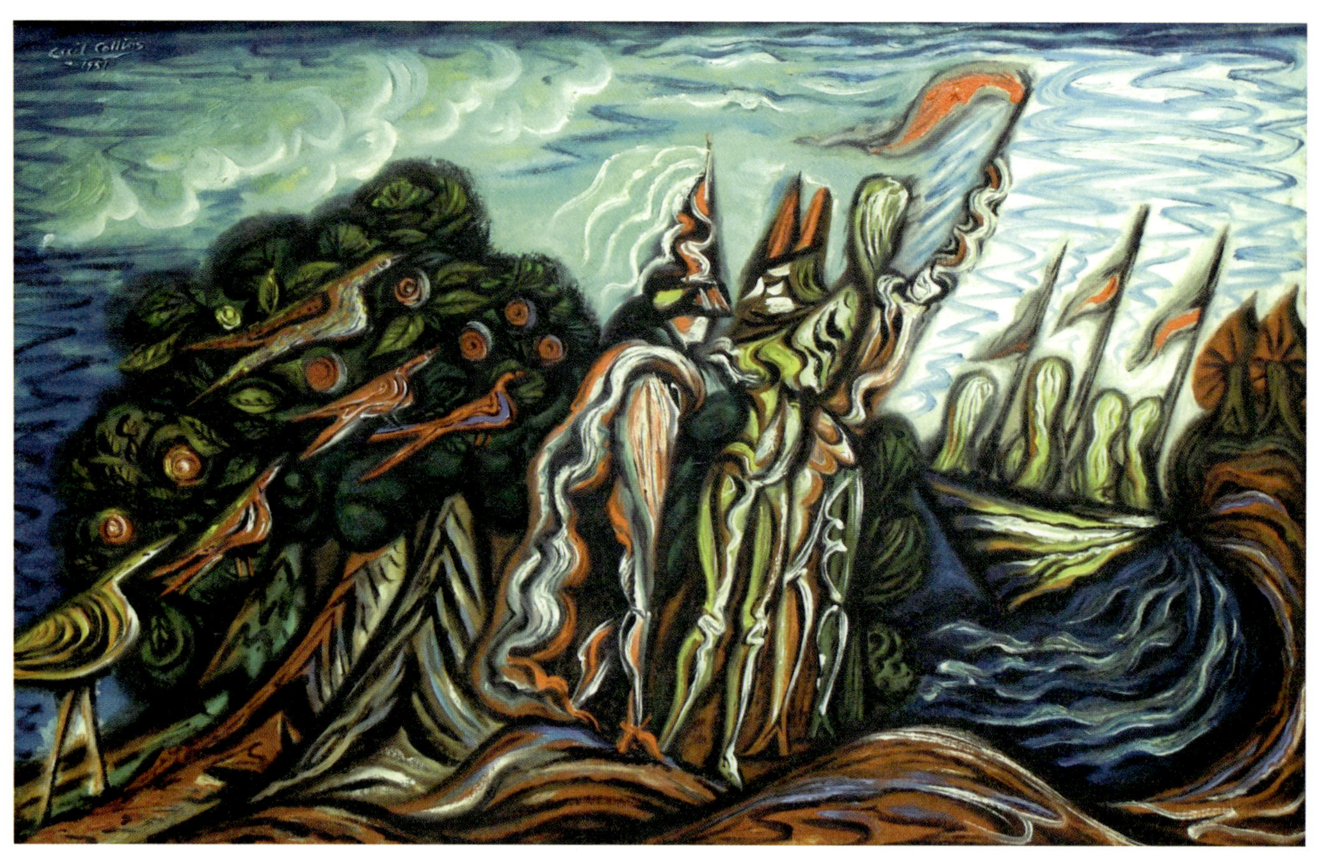

16 *Fêtes galantes* 1951
oil on canvas, 76.5 × 116

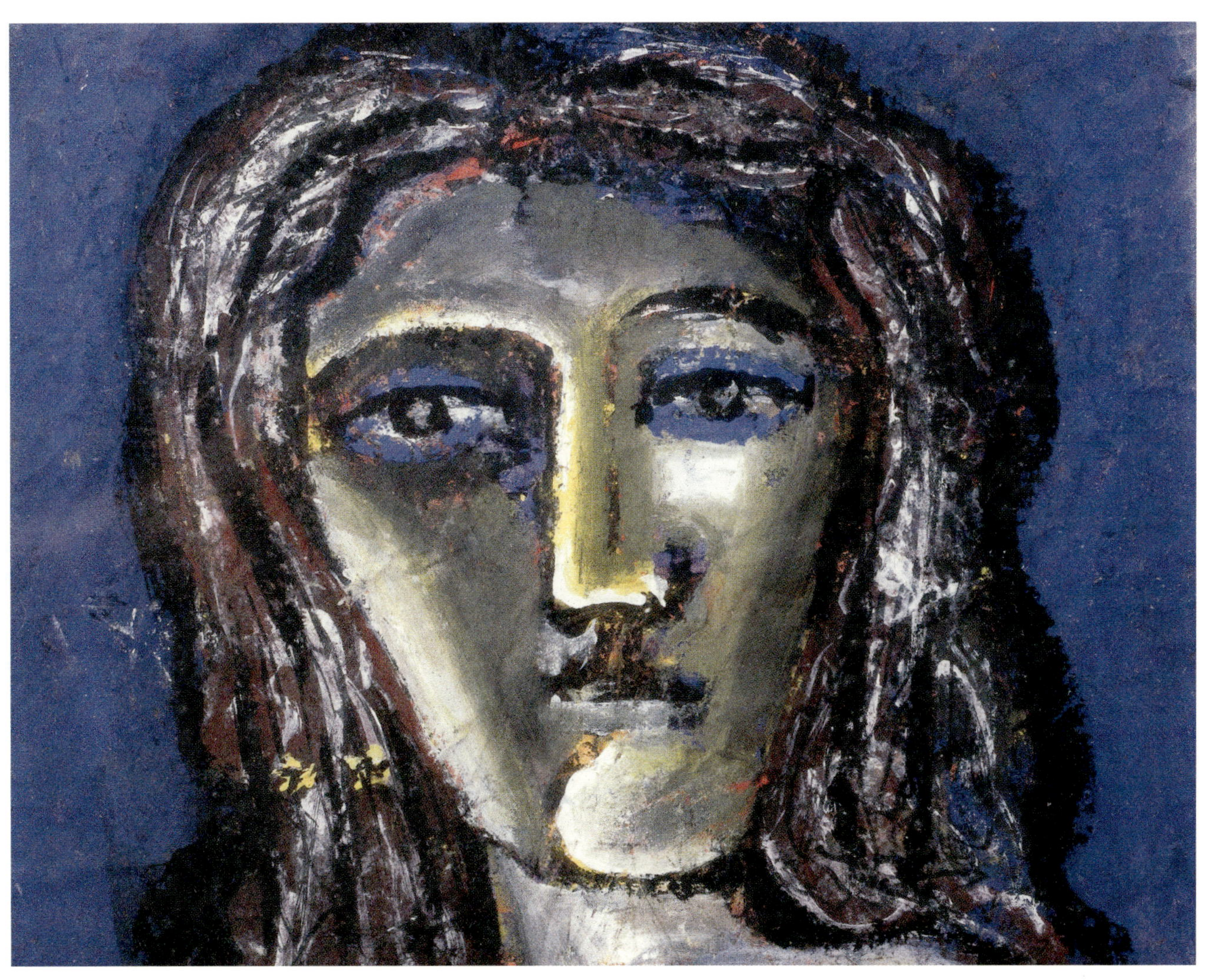

17 Head 1952
gouache, 22.5 × 26.5

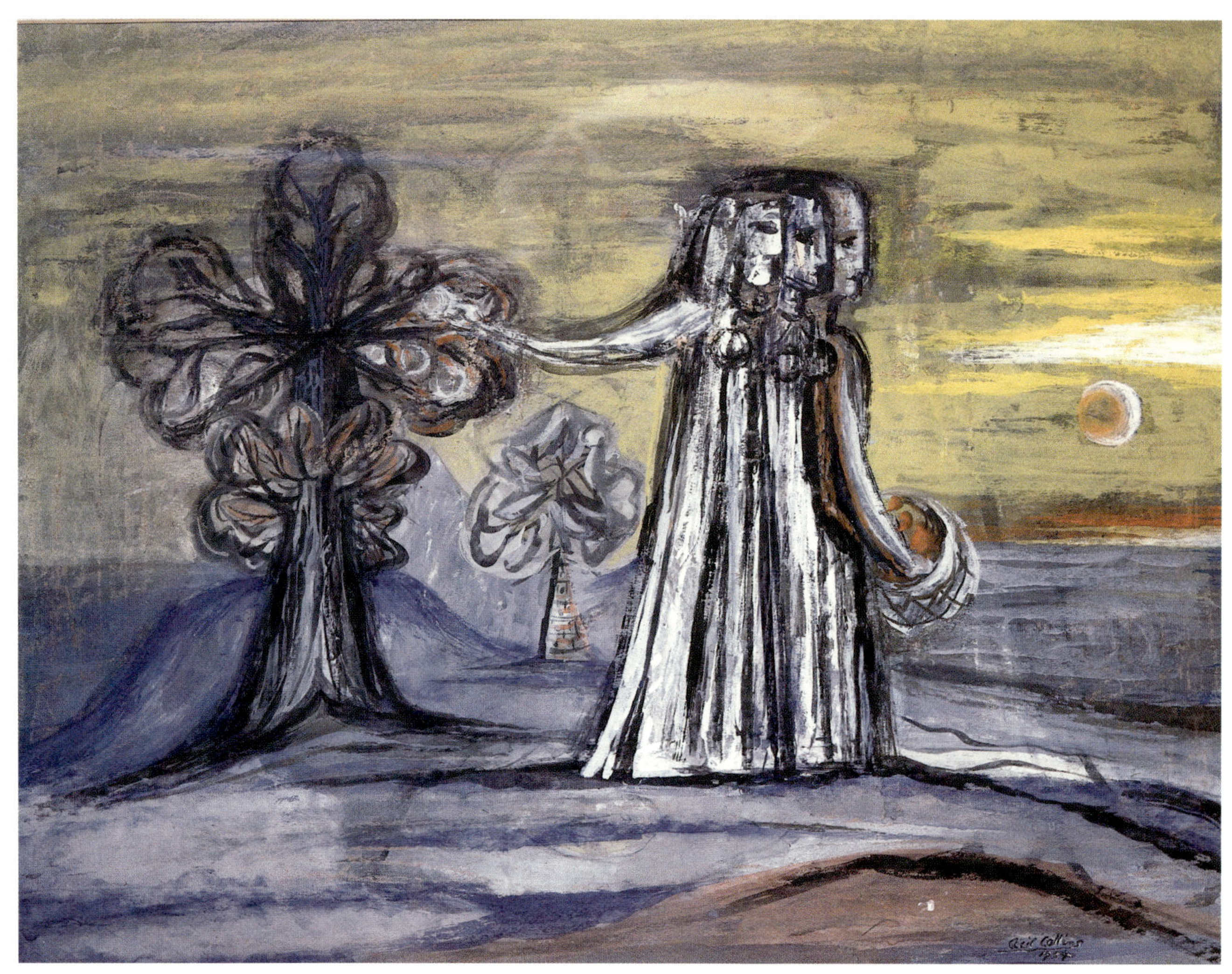

18 Figures by the Seashore   1954

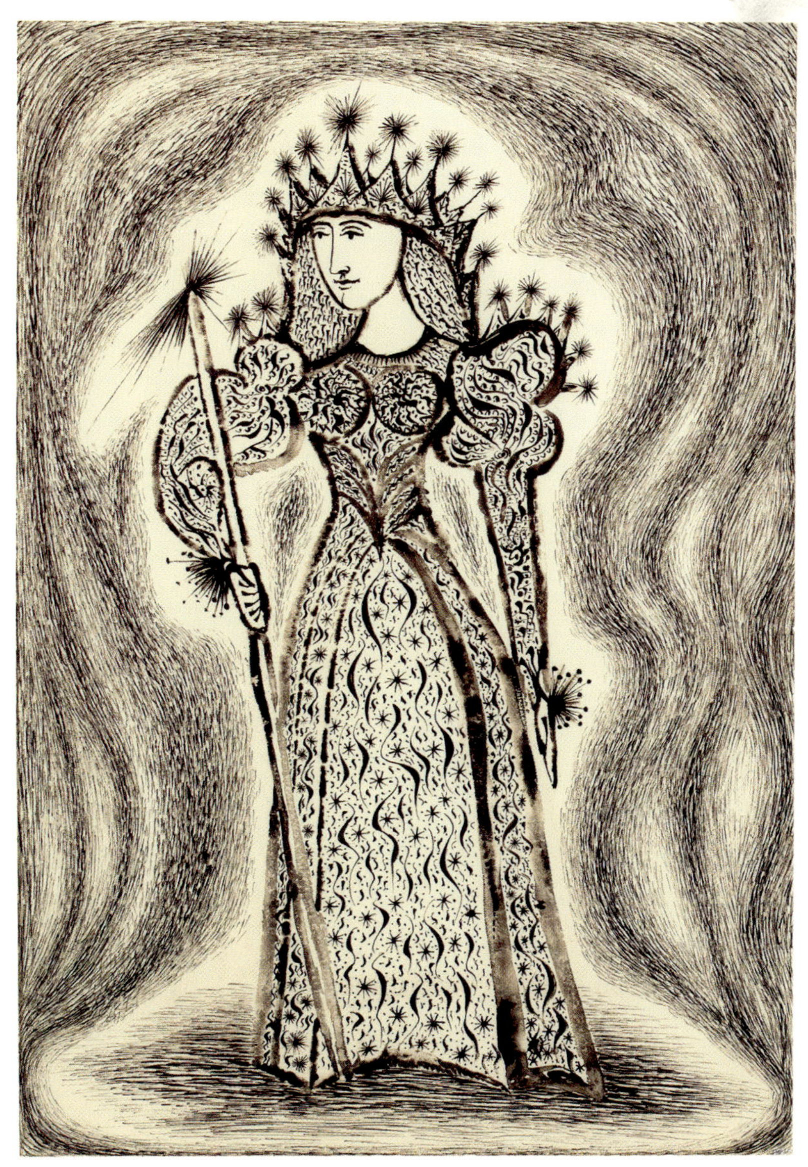

19 Queen Titania 1959
ink and wash on paper, 76 × 39.5
(One of a series of eight Shakespearean figure studies for curtain fabric 'Avon'
for the British Embassy in Washington, US)

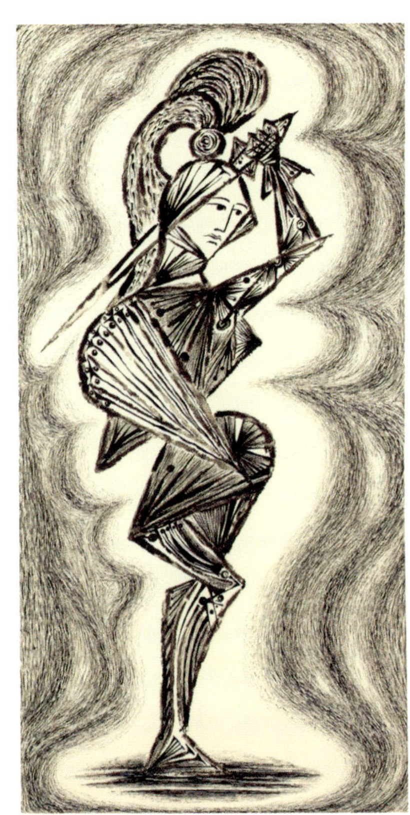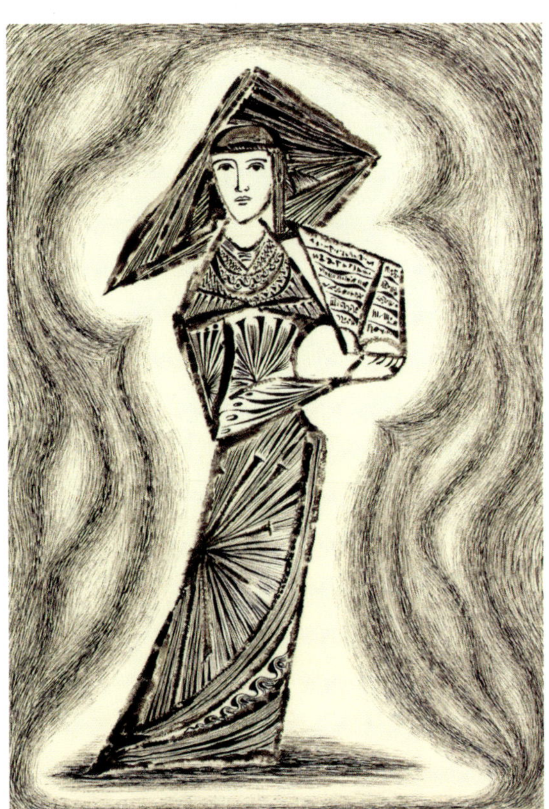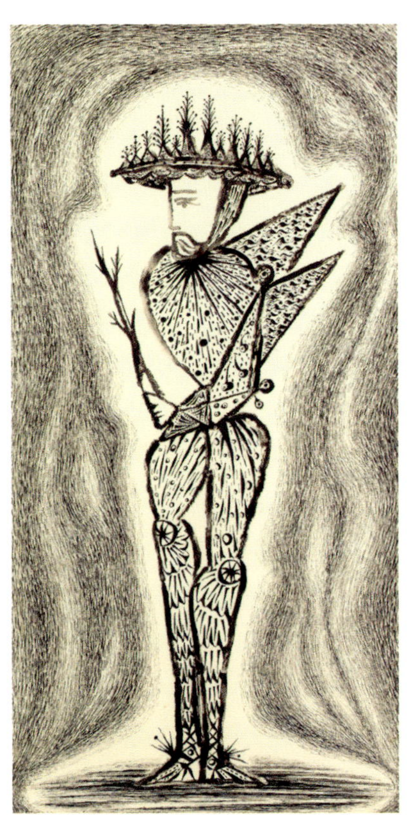

20 *Henry V, Portia, Oberon* 1959
ink and wash on paper
(see plate 19)

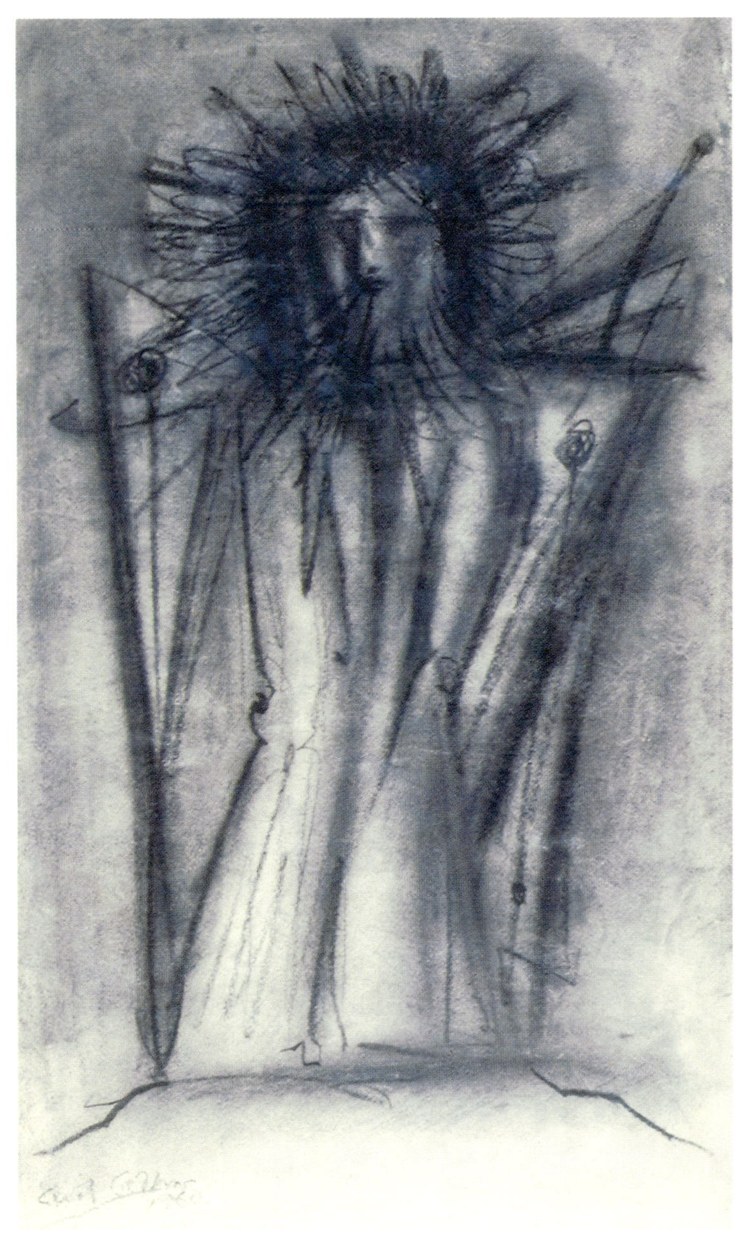

21 Angel 1960
charcoal, 37 × 22

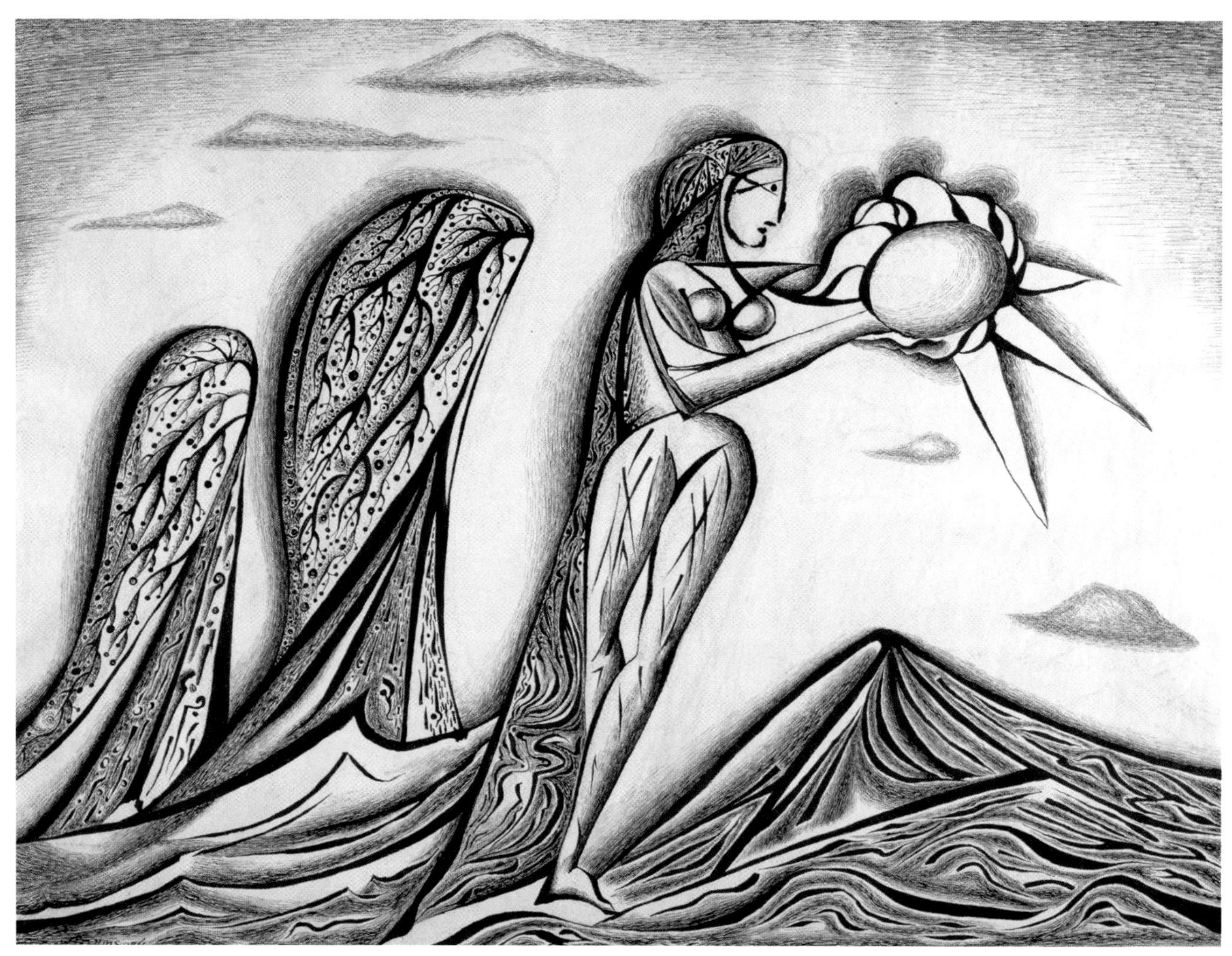

22 *Sun Bearer* 1961
pen, brush and indian ink, 56.5 × 76.2

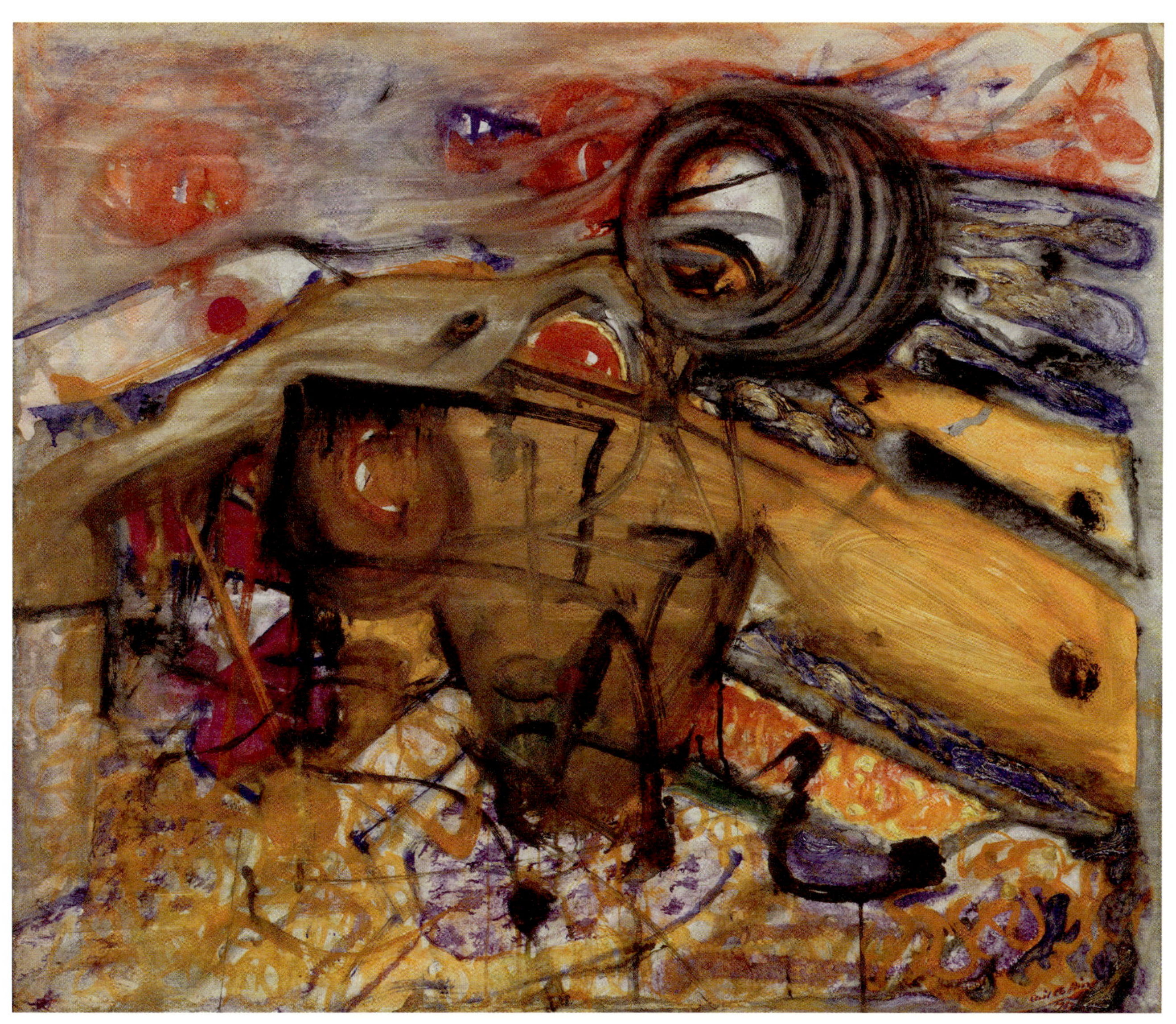

23 *Lyric Landscape* 1962
oil on board, 106 × 122

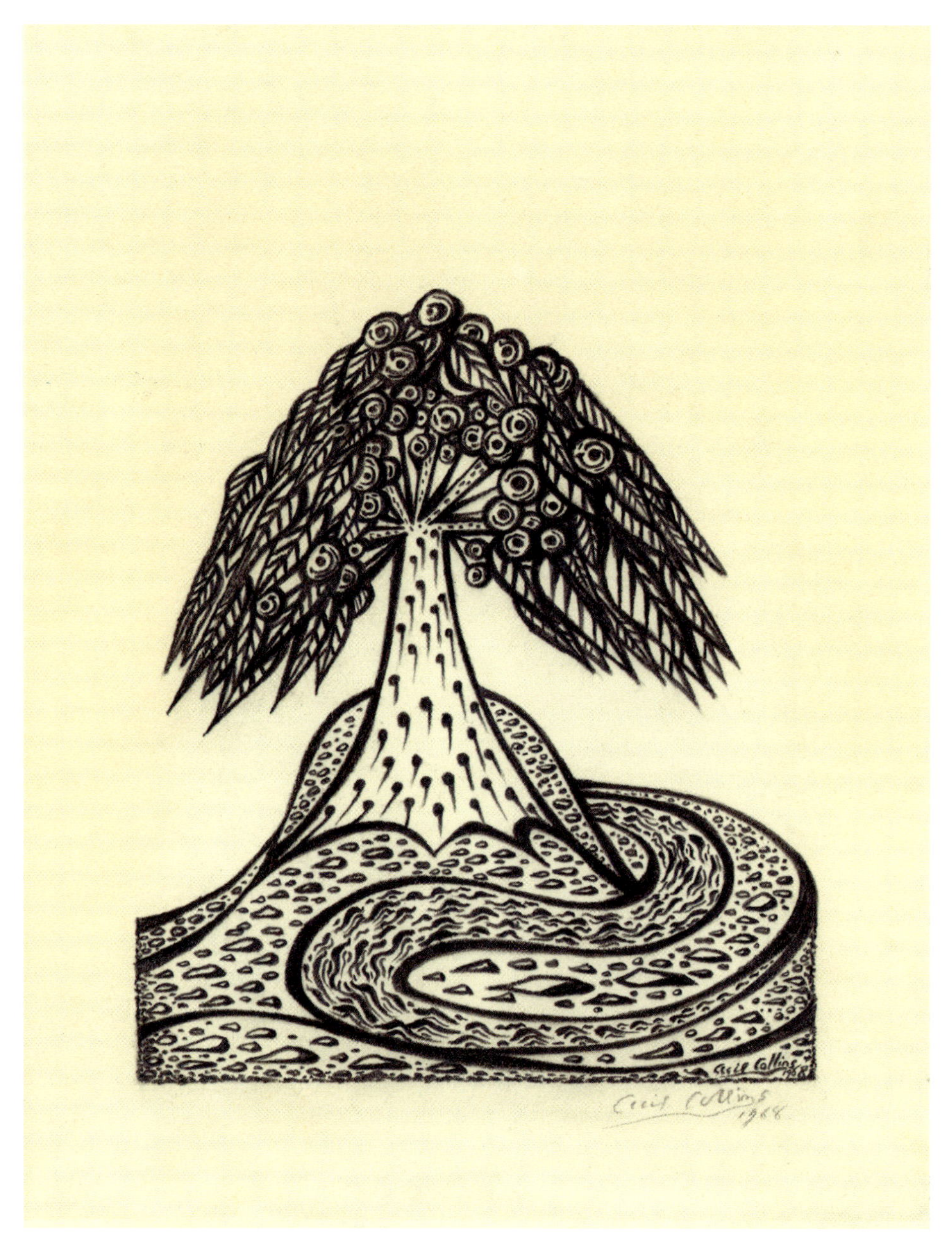

24 [*The Tree of Life*] 1968
pencil, on paper, 17 × 14.5

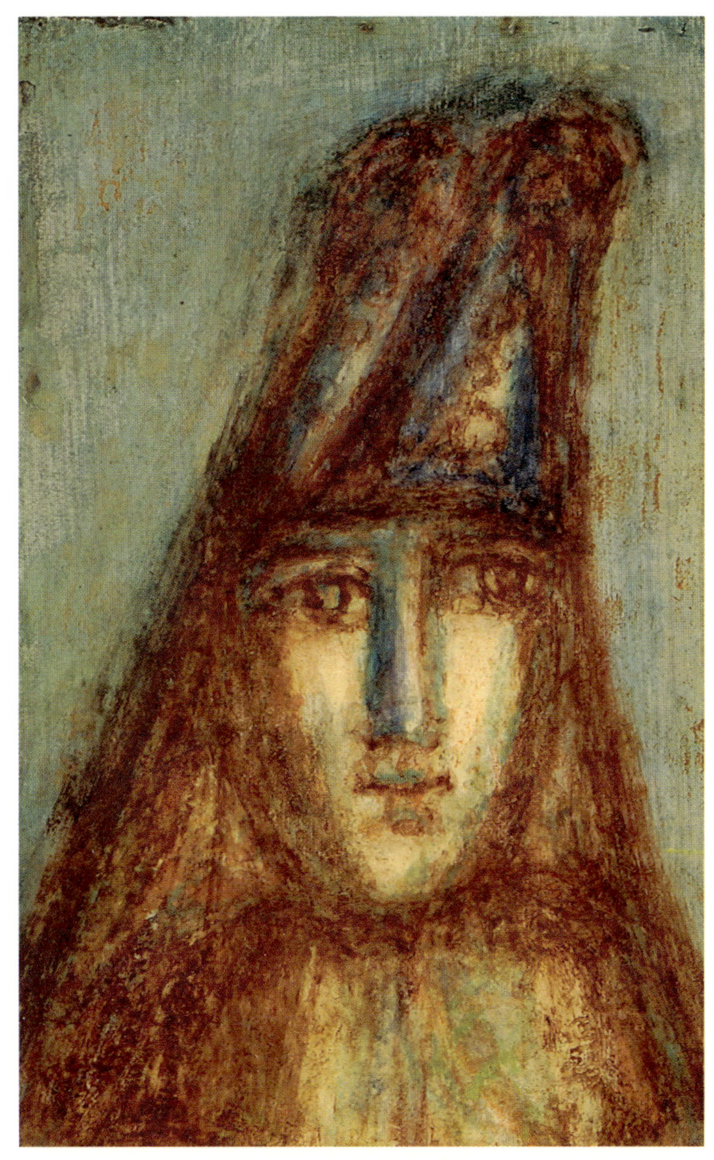

25 *Head of Fool* 1970
oil and tempera on board, 15 × 10

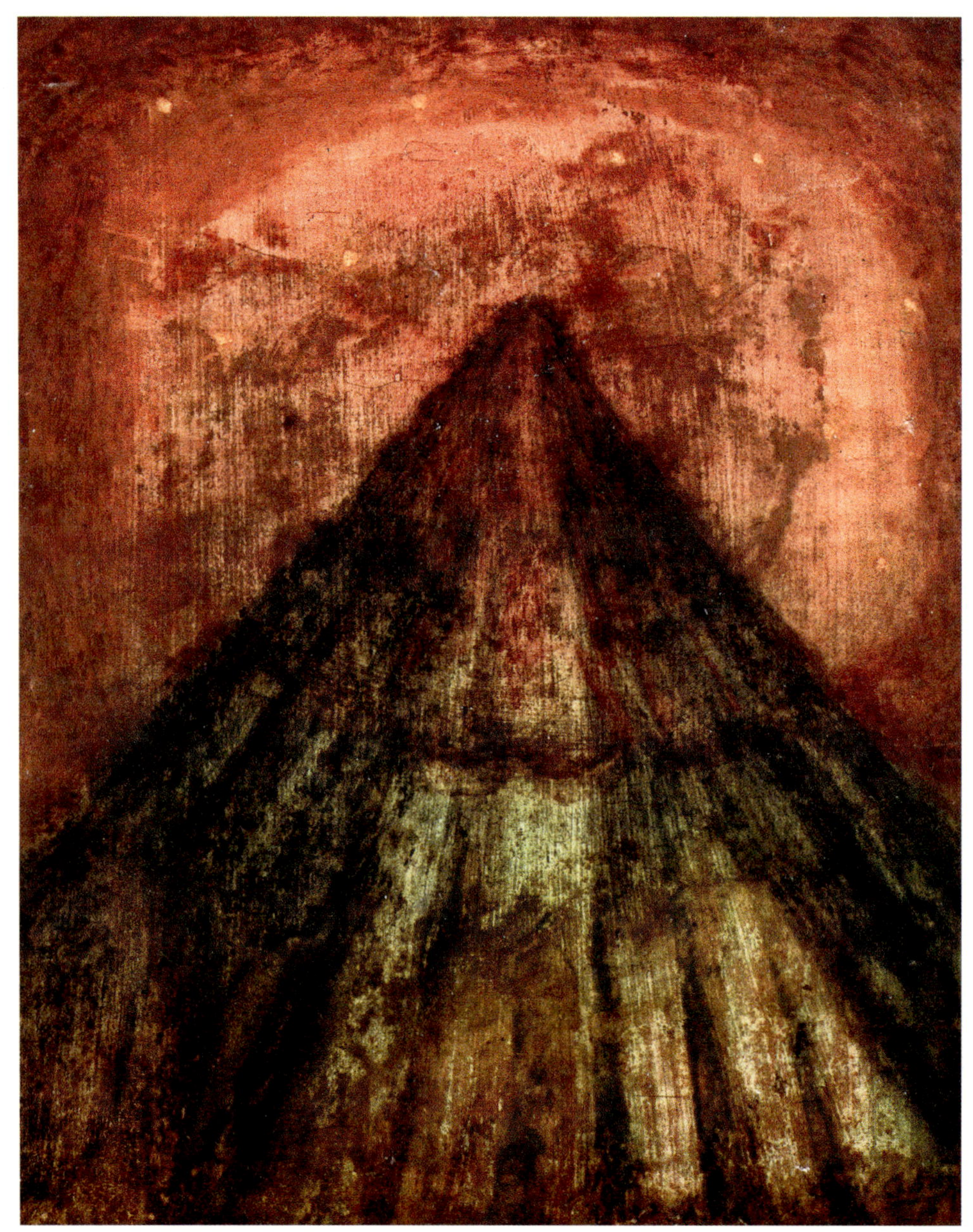

26 *The Mountain* 1973
[oil and laquer on board]

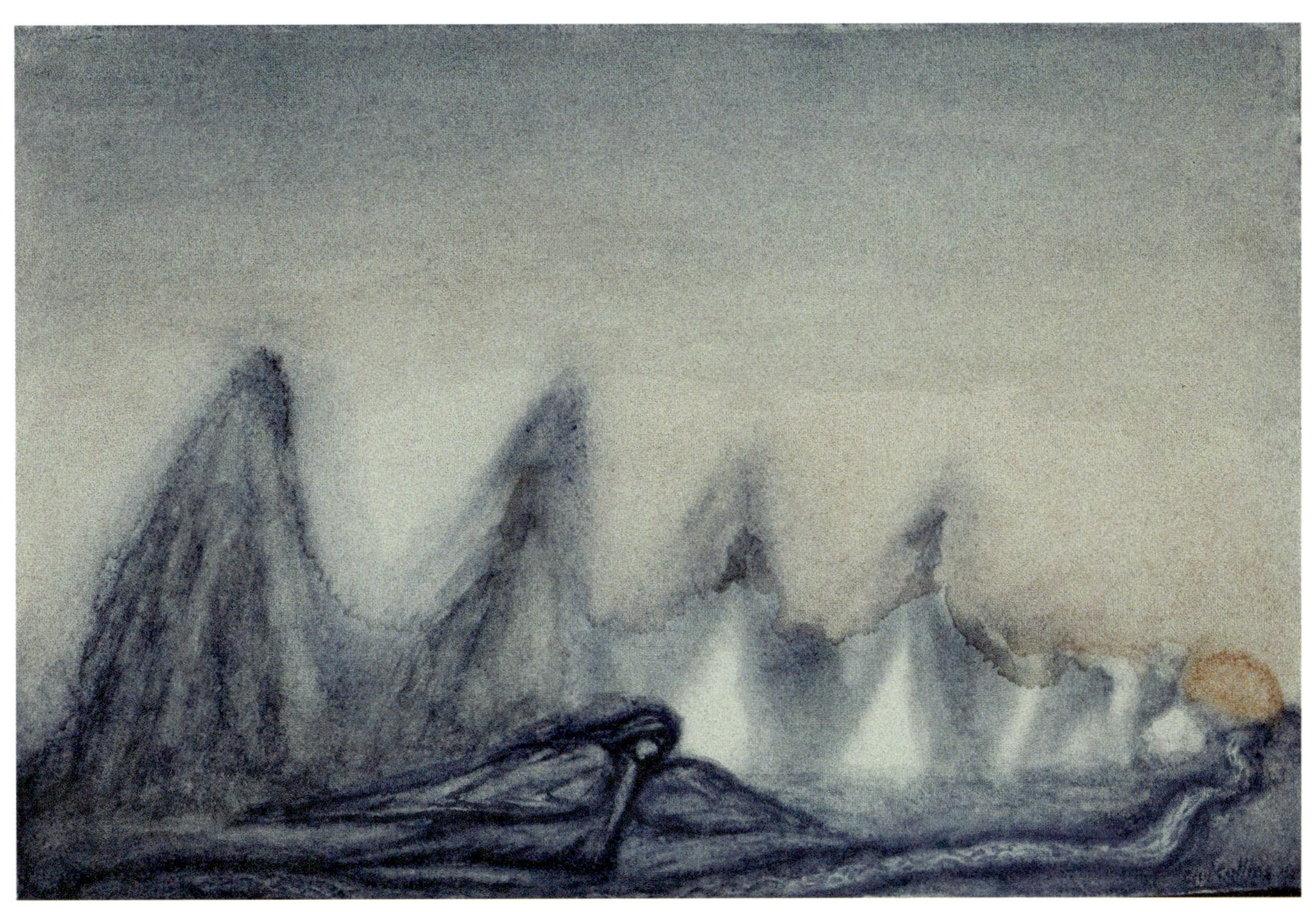

27 [*Angel in Landscape   1970s*
watercolour on paper]

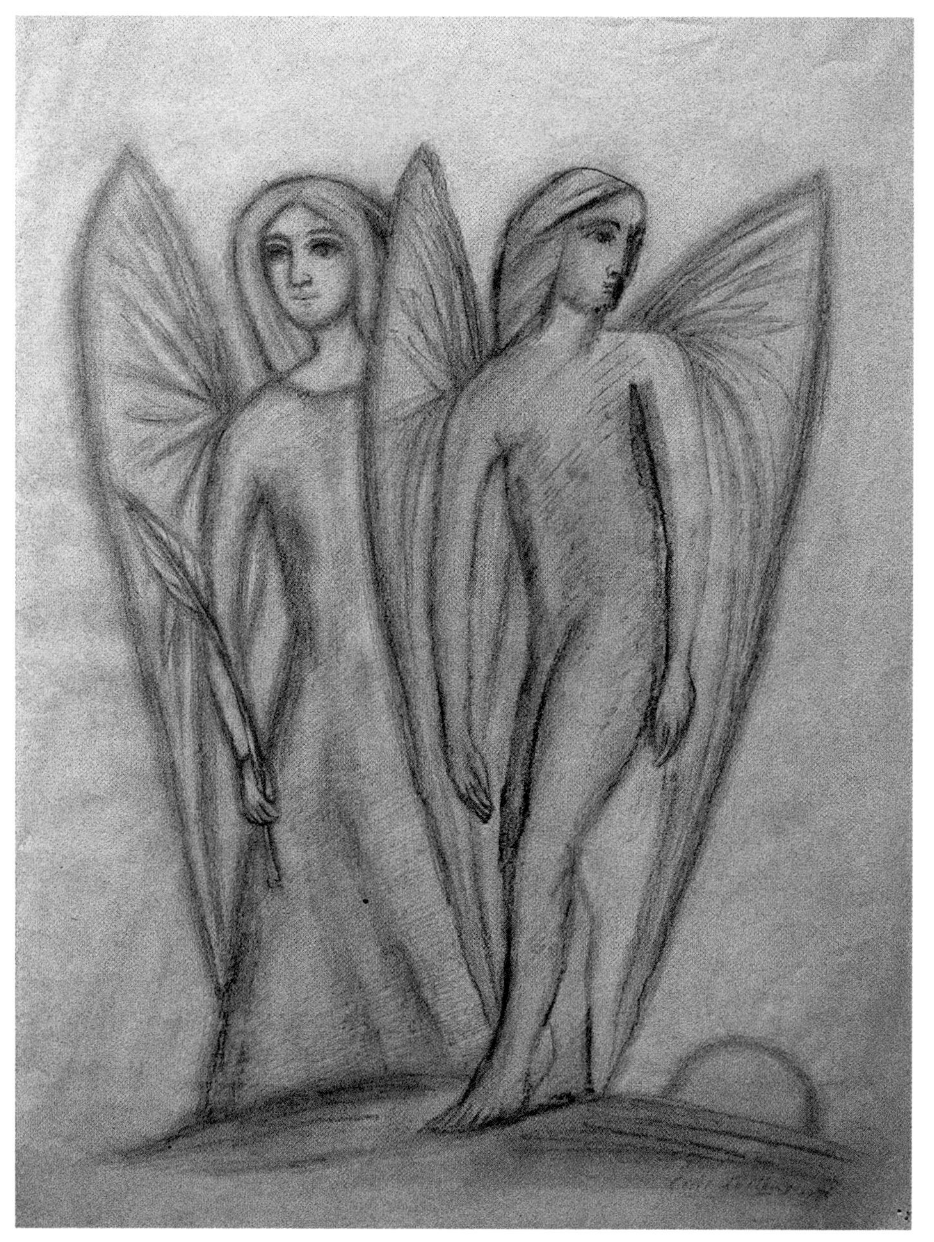

28 [Two Angels] 1976
pencil on paper

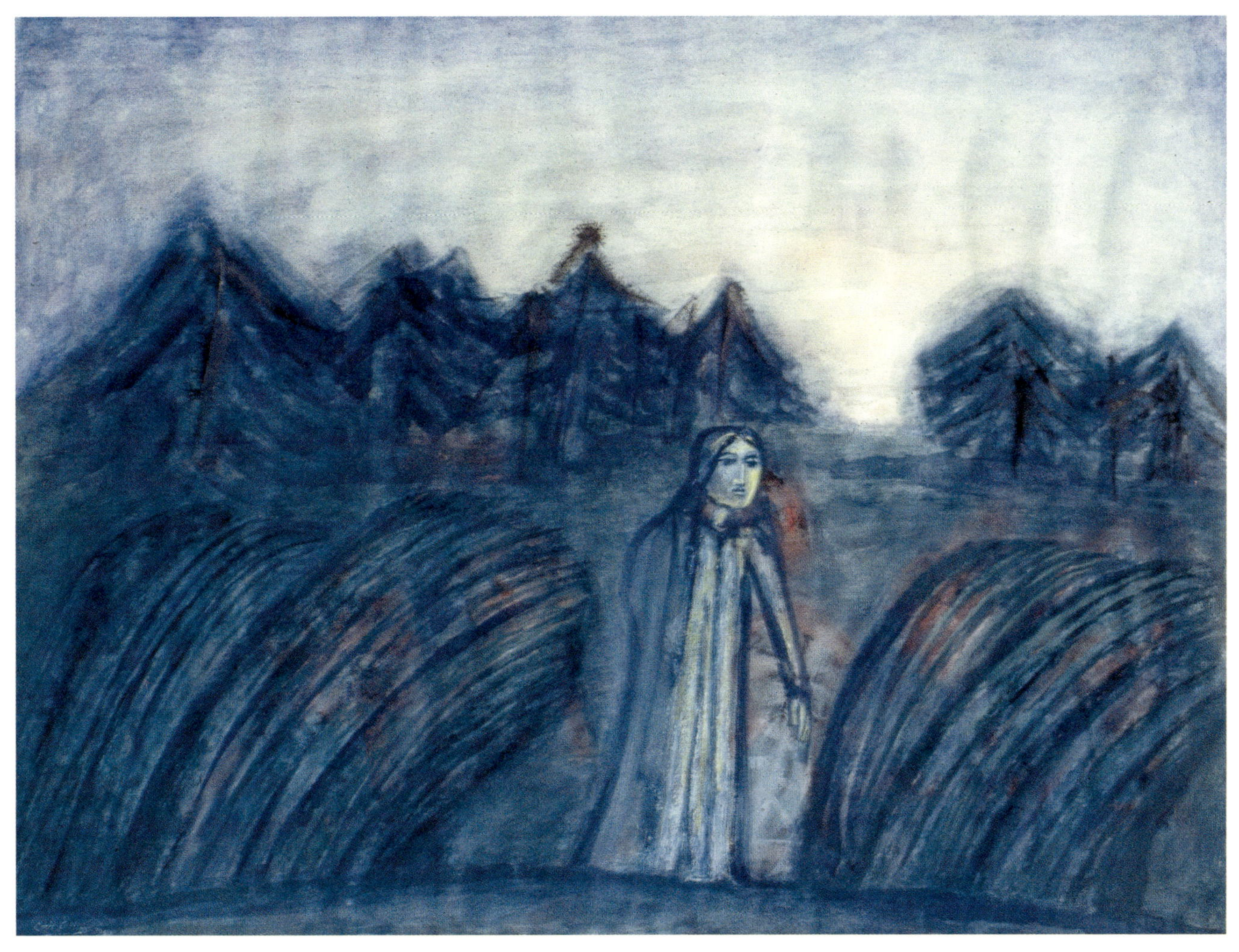

29 [*Figure in Landscape 1970s*]
gouache on paper

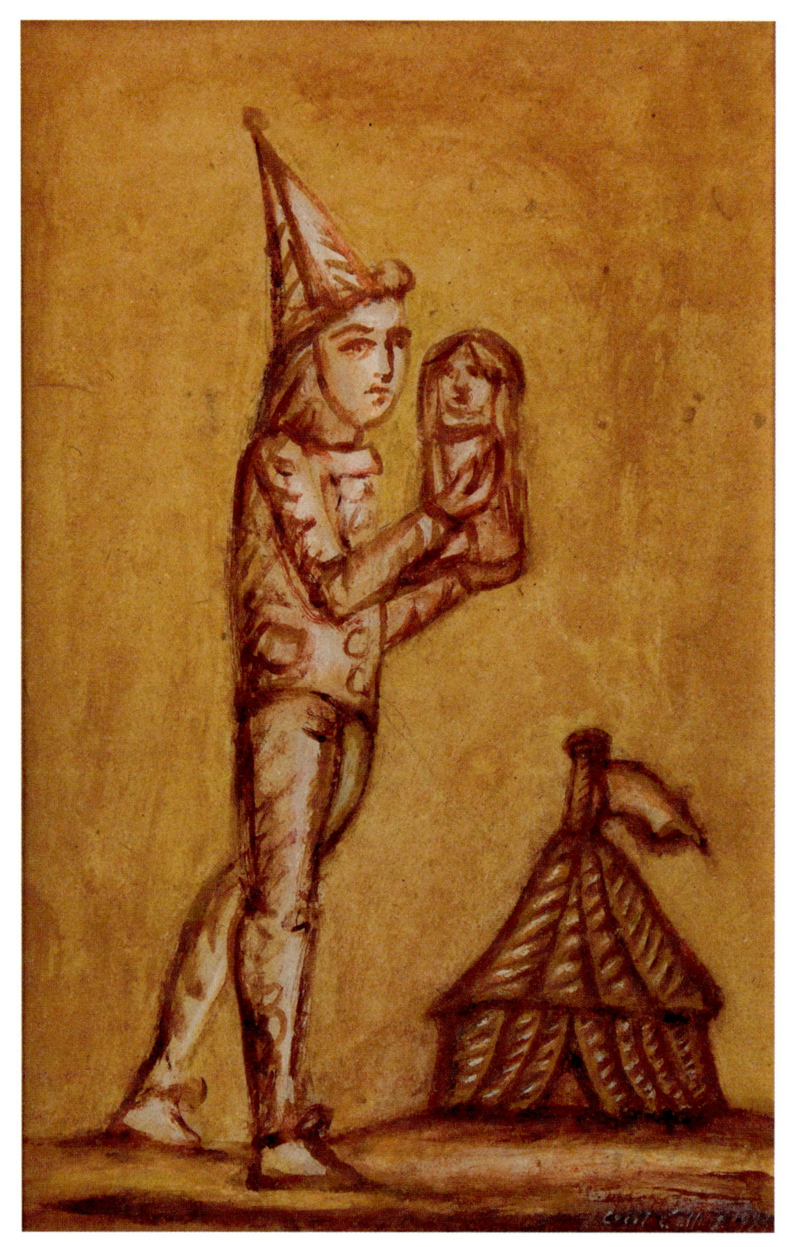

30 *Fool Carrying a Child* 1983
gouache and laquer on board, 21 × 13.5

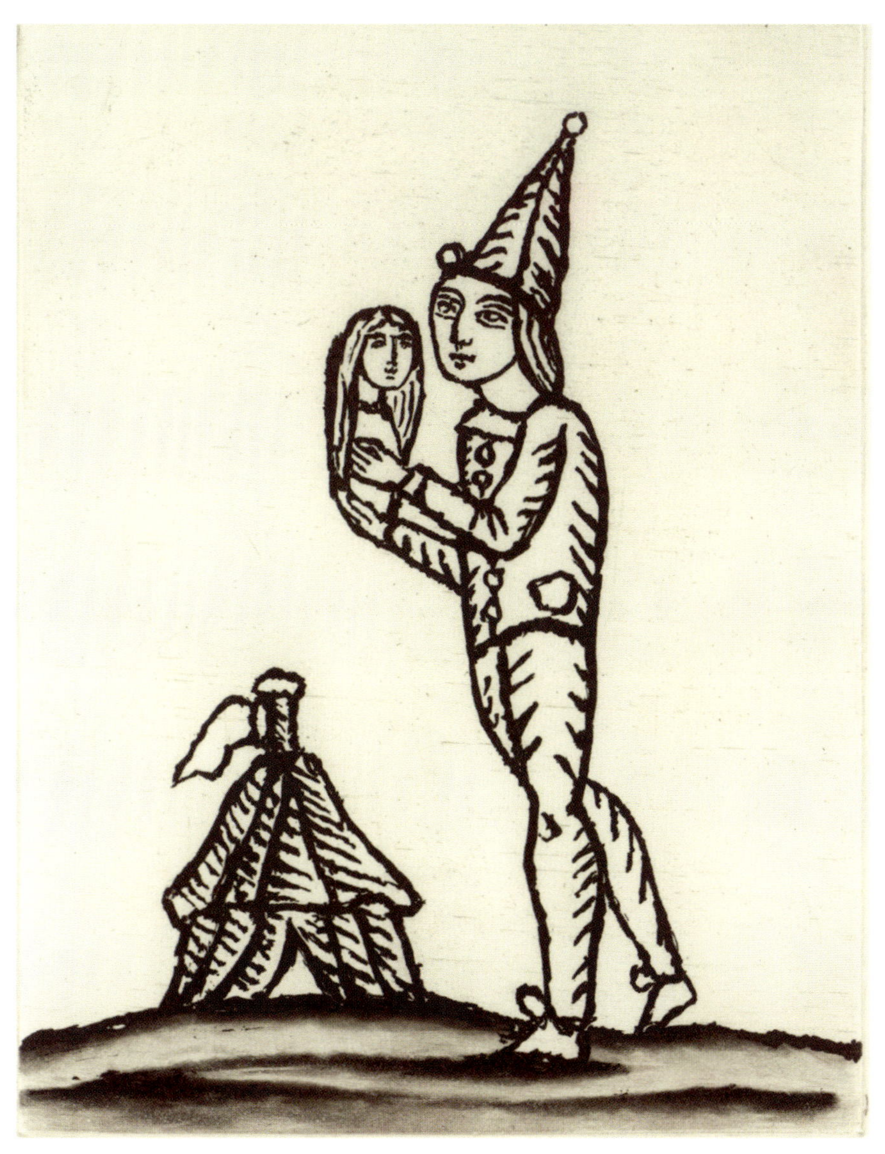

31 *Fool Carrying a Child* artist's proof, signed 1987
etching on paper, 15 × 11.5

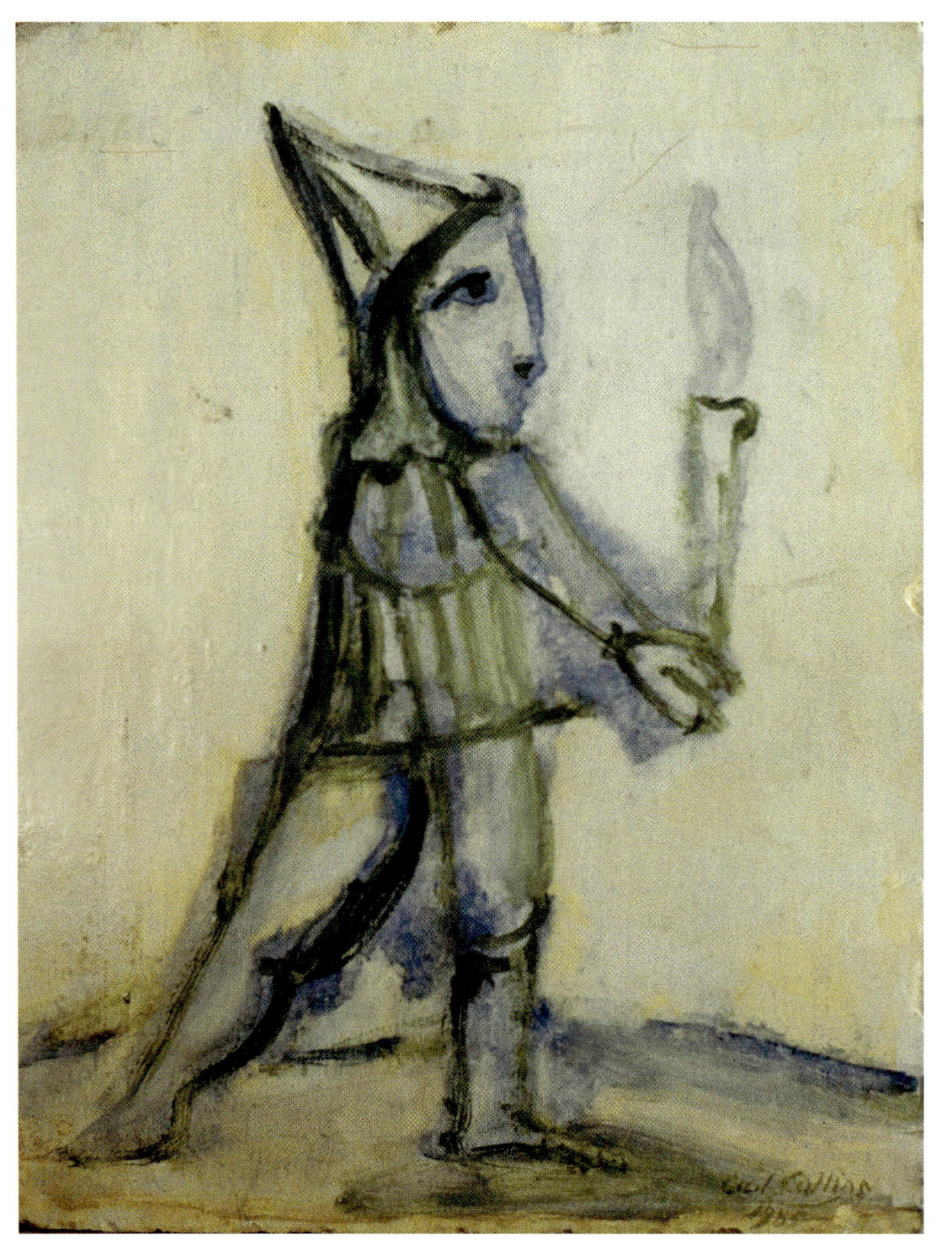

32 [*Fool with Candle* 1985
oil and laquer on board]

forms and outlines we might want to transpose either from nature or from the work of other artists. Given the recurrent figure of the Fool (never female), whether caressing a bird, at prayer, or dancing the naked joy of his innocence, we should have no interval to clothe him with our presuppositions. In his gesture is the fecundity of the Spirit; at his touch the flower breathes forth its perfume; by his sight the bird discovers the colour of its plumage; by his kneeling the landscape is sanctified. His is no physical form. Clothed in the 'fantastic garments of love', beneath which there is no muscle or bone, there is nothing that could deceive us into imagining that his presence suffers the weight of corporeality, the obligations of a physical exertion. But we discern, none the less, qualities that inform the human: movement, rhythm, tenderness, elegance, gaiety. We see all this brilliantly realised in the pencil drawing *Two Fools Dancing* of 1976 (*V.* plate 42) and, by means of the calligraphic pen, in *Fools Embracing* of 1942. (plate 4)

Such qualities transform the pen or brush stroke into a living reality. The Fool, no less than his companions in other works, is a 'station of transmission'. That is to say each pictorial image is the nodal point at which multiple levels of meaning cohere in the nuance of line, colour and shape. By this configuration on the picture surface they have their life and confront us as transforming agents of consciousness. In the bending of the Fool to touch the flower is the moment of benediction in which we apprehend the grace that is bestowed by the unity of inner and outer natures. The specific beauty of the painted image is the occasion of our recognition that the division of subject from object is already the tool of a reductive consciousness; as if through that beauty unity of being was able to fulfil itself.

Often we are given only the head of the Fool, in whose self-contained, dispassionate gaze is condensed the mystery of our birth into consciousness– our coming into being. The Fool's melancholy and openness are never wholly revealed in any one painting. His impersonal life is partly lived in all the other pictures in which he is present, each appearance implied in every other. This characteristic is shared by the whole of Collins's work. Each Angel is one of a community of Angels; each Pilgrim journeys part of the way that is only fully undertaken in the cumulative journey of each and every Pilgrim; each Sibyl, emissary of the unknown, utters her prophecy as the fragment of an omniscience known only to all Sibyls together. Each painting and drawing is a window onto a continually unfolding vision, inexhaustible in its nature. This characteristic of the artist's work is perhaps most fully realised in *The Invocation* of 1944 (V. plate 6), where the feminine figure, at once bride, sybil, prophetess and emblem of the spirit of creativity, is in total responsive fecundity with the landscape she both creates and blesses, even as she is part of it. Indeed, the picture in its totality is a richly articulated transmutation of the artistic process itself.

All of which might suggest that the pictures themselves are effete, sapped of the reality proper to them as works rendered in paint or pencil, like rarefied ghosts of their maker's consciousness. But the artist has complete technical mastery of every medium he works with. Each picture, whether in ink, paint, pencil or whatever, displays an artist's proper concern and delight in the properties of his chosen medium. How could it be otherwise? No artist could adequately express such a depth of resonance as is here were he not able to take it for granted that no privation or hindrance would be imposed on him by his own technical insufficiency. It is a consequence of Collins's mastery that each picture lives only in the medium in which it is created. He very seldom made preparatory studies for his paintings. For this reason (at least in part) you could not transpose a drawing, for instance, to the medium of paint without destroying the specific life of the image that is drawn, so indissoluble is the bond between applied technique and the realization of the image. We see this is the two images of a Fool carrying a Child (plates 30 and 31) where the pictorial motif is duplicated (even if reversed as a composition), but where each image is wholly present only in the medium of its creation. Despite the similarity, each has an autonomous substantial life. There can be no question of a squared drawing being scaled up to become a larger painted image. Recessed beyond layer after layer of pigment and lacquer, can we say that this head – Fool or Anima, or even numinous Mountain (see plate 26) – is other than the physical substance of its rendering? Is the image given birth from the medium; has the artist been taken unawares as the worked substance congealed into a living presence? Or, in the dry austerity of tempera, could it be that the tree, the bird and the woman were already alive under the surface leaving the painter with only the task of brushing away the covering that veils their presence? In the final analysis, moment of vision and rendered image, like the dancer and the dance, have no life apart from one another, each painted and drawn image intuits the miraculous gift of incarnation.

Collins's compelling technical mastery, both as colourist and as draughtsman, is never deployed for its own sake. He has spoken of such vacuity as producing 'visual confectionery'. For him technique has its own meditative content. How else are we to understand that an art devoted to invoking the spontaneity of intuitive consciousness should proceed by means of techniques that are as often as not deliberately slow and painstaking in their execution? In his compositions Collins puts aside the more customary architectonic devices for ordering the picture plane. Instead, an almost musical notation comes into play, so that we find a picture is formally organized through the counterpoint of his characteristic visual rhymes, thematic repetitions, and carefully modulated tonal ranges of colour with harmonic complements and discordant clashes.

In *Hymn to Night* (1951), a typical example, the depth and benevolence of ultramarine and cobalt collects and interiorizes our gaze, taking it inwards to a landscape in the foreground of which a feminine figure is poised by a tree. The one articulated rhythm of life's energy is echoed throughout, flowing down the hair, then up the tree trunk, then spread abundantly in the leaves no less than in the river that flows in the middle distance. The seeming mirror image of the woman's crossed hands is echoed repeatedly, as if from a pivotal point, in the dual image of the tree's foliage, an angel's wings, the raised wings of several swans and in the branches of the trees that cover a distant hill. Within the narrow spectrum of colour, woman and landscape are possessed of a single tonal being. This is the case also in *Figure in a Landscape*, for instance. (plate 29)

In *Daybreak* (1971; V. plate 18) is the burden of hope that is present in green. Beyond the turbulent energy of generative waves, already receding before the onlooker, three feminine figures emerge from a placid sea. They proffer a token of new birth in the shape of a flowering plant whose blooms are already vivified with the chrome of the rising sun. A bird, emblem of the soul, held by one of the figures, has its eyes fixed resolutely on the horizon, its breast, like those of the three faces, kindled by the sun's light.

In *Wounded Angel* (1967; V. plate 15) the harmonic interval from orange to violet offers its sanctuary to an Angel which, in the lightness of its being, has returned to rest on the floor of Paradise, exhausted from the effort of witnessing the self-disfiguration of man's forgetfulness of the divine. In the drawings, the dynamism and energy of the theme is often paradoxically enhanced by means of techniques that, as we have already noted, are evidently laborious and exact, the result of a meticulous application of thousands of single strokes of the pen or pencil, as in, for instance, *The Resurrection* of 1952. (V. plate 37) This same technique is also used in the pen drawings that are prepatory studies for the curtain fabric *Avon* of 1959. (p. 32, and plates 19 and 20)

The principal images in which Collins's vision is focused are the trinity of Fool, Angel and feminine Anima. About the Fool the artist has himself spoken in detail in his manifesto *The Vision of the Fool*. The Fool affirms purity of consciousness. Simple, innocent, vulnerable, the Fool bequeaths to us the ultimate freedom of our identity and destiny. His joy and essence are that charity of the heart that in love and beauty redeems the politics of time.

The winged Angel, agent of transformation and the divine wisdom, an intermediary of Truth, seeks only to awaken our assent. Ever watchful, guardian, guide, judge, the Angel, as companion to the Fool, is always about some action–its presence always purposeful, if not directive–its role to pierce with the divine brightness the darkening substance that is the desolation of this world.

The Anima, Eternal Bride, often only a head, has a complex role. By contrast with Fool and Angel she is unmoving, rejecting nothing, vigilant, uncensorious; she reflects in her wise compassion an absorbed, unfathomable passivity. She is the subjective pole of the moment of intuitive imagination, the masculine pole of which is fixed by the process of visualization which is the act of making these visionary images as objects. In virtue of the complementarity of these two poles the whole realm of Collins's art comes into existence. This situation is analogous to the traditional symbolism of the *animus*, masculine spirit, and *anima*, feminine soul, who, in their inter-relationship generate the world in so far as it is objectively knowable. Priestess and guardian, un-maternal, none the less from Collins's eternal feminine all actions flow and to her enduring benediction they return. In her is mirrored the mysterious depth of the human universe as an image of contemplation.

Cecil Collins's isolation as an artist is due not only to the unexpected nature of his visual language, but also to the fact that an imaginative vision such as his is without protection in the cultural consensus of modernism, to which it is a reproach. As if in answer to some inevitable summons, some objectifying instinct, and against the resistance of a malaise and a blindness, these images have been conjured into existence to pose the metaphysical imperative to an age mesmerized by the surface of things. They are like the seeds of what must grow to take the place of this malaise and blindness. The artist's imaginative vision, which has no concern for the substance of history, by a telling paradox has about it the savour of historical necessity. For the beauty and the serenity of these images comprehend the true measure of our cultural exhaustion. In them we are finally given some purchase against the successive depredations of the secular, self-disfiguring patterns of our culture. In them we witness emblems of our true humanity as it is renewed and refreshed in the sacred unknown.

*

This modest two-part essay cannot hope to come to anything more than a provisional conclusion about the final merit of Cecil Collins's achievement. Even if such a thing were possible, that was never the intention. From the outset we have been concerned primarily to act as a guide towards an authentic approach to what must come first: a proper understanding of the artist's goal. This, as I hope I have shown, entails our acceptance that his art rests upon a body of intellectual and spiritual premises that are far from those which underpin the norms of modern thought and culture. Without at least recognizing the necessity of this approach, any critical assessment of his work will have no integral foundation on which to proceed, let alone reach a conclusion. After all – of whatever stature – all art is only meaningful and of value within a given cultural context. A good deal of this context, in Collins's case, is provided by his own written record. I have mostly extrapolated from that.

Cecil Collins was a child of the twentieth century, so much so that, inescapably, his formulation of the place of art in human life, as well as his actual practice as a maker of images, involved him in adopting certain of the features of his age. He was not, after all, entirely free from subscribing to the humanist idea of 'creativity' as an end in itself; a creative freedom that seeks to give an absolute value to artistic expression whilst at the same time, in practice, removing it step by step and over several centuries from the over-arching context of the intellectual, spiritual and ethical principles we invoke whenever the question of grasping the deepest import of a work of art is in question.

It is possible that, in the final analysis, an eventual conclusion will be that Collins attempted the impossible: that his avowed intent to give pictorial expression to a transcendent vision was in the end too mitigated by incommensurable factors. We have seen how the artist, steeped in the wisdom of the sacred traditions, understood how art can be an adjunct to the realization of their respective spiritual possibilities. And as we hinted at the end of the first part of this essay, such is the artist's commitment to this view of art in relation to spirituality that it becomes inescapable that his own art must be evaluated in terms of how art might function as a support for effective contemplation. This in turn amounts to admitting that art must be integral to a more encompassing metaphysical, cosmological and symbolic framework. Whether this can be achieved outside of the canonical context of a given religious tradition remains an open question. Perhaps the most profound question that the arts have been faced with in recent centuries is: to what extent can art serve genuine spiritual attainment whilst adopting features of a non- or quasi-religious aesthetic?

But all this is a long way off in respect of a comprehensive judgement of Collins's achievement. In the meantime, we must come to know and love the best of his work, see clearly the terms by which it succeeds as well as fails and only then, in our response, acknowledge, as I believe, that such works (that rarest of attainments) resonate with a beauty which touches infallibly upon the eternal order of reality. In granting this much we might also recognize that that beauty has the power to vanquish the idea that art has no greater purpose than to provoke the more evanescent facets of subjective experience.

The Anatomy of the Fool
by Cecil Collins

Some years ago, when preparing a collected edition of Cecil Collins's writings, I took the decision not to include the text that follows, first published in Transformation, No. 3 (pp. 25–28), 1945. I thought at the time that it would be an unnecessary duplication of the slightly later text of The Vision of the Fool, *the 'manifesto' of the artist's oeuvre, first published, with illustrations, as a book in 1947. Rereading the 'Anatomy' I now see that this is not an entirely defendable judgement. As one might expect, this text does not say anything radically different from the slightly later 'manifesto'. There is no textual overlap, so that the 'Anatomy' does not read like a draft of the 'manifesto', being a self-contained, succinct and decisive expression of the artist's primary imaginative motif. It is presumably the artist's earliest attempt to conceptualize the central symbol of his thought and iconography, giving emphasis to the importance of the symbol of the Fool as it applies to contemporary cultural and social conditions, as well as expressing what the inner necessity of the symbol signifies for the artist himself. I have included it here so that it might add its own value to the present context.*

. . . And so in 1940 I commenced my series of paintings and drawings called 'The Holy Fools', and for the next five years concentrated upon them. Not because I had a definite concept of the Fool, and then worked to that; no, what happened was, that as I worked on the paintings, a realization of what the Fool really meant and signified grew gradually and naturally in me. Many years later, through studying and looking at the paintings, I at last began to understand a little the significance of the Fool; it was the paintings that expressed and revealed it to me. The idea of the Fool had, of course, been strongly with me many years before I commenced my paintings; but not as a concept, it was as a particular quality of emotion, generated by the experience of being alive, and by contemplating the spectacle of contemporary society.

The Fool became one of the most significant images in the mythology of my painting, the Fool was the one complete symbol which could contain and sum up all that I believed and sensed to be creative and alive in that vast desert of machines which has been called, rather ambitiously, civilization. The symbol deepened for me when I realized more and more the universality of the Fool's nature. A symbol that can exist in all religions and yet be detached from them. A symbol that can take on the local colour of religions and societies and yet remain pure in essence. This purity of essence which is the universality of the Fool's nature, is one of the factors that provides structure to society; for it is integrity, not the integrity of following some intellectual idea or concept but the integrity of life itself. And in that deep-rooted integrity the anatomy of the Fool reveals an ironic innocence, which is formidable. This ironic innocence is a leaven which helps to bring society to fruition. The charity of the Saint, and the vision of the Artist, bring about the same fruition in different ways. The Fool is united with them, so that all their different energies meet in one flame, which is an internal ferment, causing growth in the body of human society.

It causes growth, not progress. These words are unfortunately too often confused. The only real progress is growth in wisdom. The attributes of growth exist in Art and Religion, and in that fine flower of these two rich soils, the Fool. To civilize is to cause to grow. The Fool is an internal energy in living consciousness whose potency comes from an innocence which transcends all knowledge. This energy, when it is allowed to live, stimulates growth in the society of human beings by causing an expansion and a radiance of human attitude.

The Fool has been rejected by our Age, which is a period of the subjection of the Humanities by the tyranny of one mode of thought that is Science. Human society, inasmuch as it grows in depth of wisdom, accepts the Fool. Men accept him as a mysterious, vitalizing element in life, mysterious because proceeding direct from the mystery of life itself. It is enough for such men to have this potency of life itself in the midst of their various activities of ambition, and the obsessions of commerce; without having to make the Fool fit into some mechanical scheme sufficiently obvious to satisfy the utilitarian and baser elements in man.

The potent innocence of the Fool, with the wit of his ironic compassion, excites the humanity in man to communion with the humanity in all men.

The neglect and rejection of the Fool is one of the signs that characterizes the decay of a society, no matter if that society has achieved a high degree of technical conquest in the organizing of life. For such a technical achievement, without the guidance of wisdom, remains an undeveloped form of society which has yet to become human. The aim of the process of civilization should be to transmute the species of man into a human species. A true society is the process of the metamorphosis of man into [the] human. The contemplation of the condition of the modern world is a clear proof of this. The manifest bankruptcy and sterility of contemporary society shows at last its cold white bones through the thin flesh of the talk of progress. We have developed Science higher than most other activities in our life. Scientific technics occupy more of man's consciousness than they have ever done before, and cover most of the field of his education. And yet, with all this dominance of scientific thought, we have the disaster and degradation of contemporary society. If today there had been as much wisdom as there has been Science, the war which has destroyed human standards and values of life would never have taken place. If the experience of our period in history has revealed anything at all, it has clearly shown that Science is not wisdom. Power in any other hands but those of wisdom is evil and destructive.

The forgetting of the Fool by society, and the rejection of that society by the Fool, is mutual. The Fool rejects modern society because the Fool represents that profound fertile innocence down from which we have fallen into the dirt and filth of mechanical existence. Society thought that it could live without the foundation of the deep-rooted integrity of this essential innocence. It then gradually began to forget the life of this quality of the mind and the spirit until eventually the Fool had for society little or no existence at all. The society of men, therefore, has forgotten the elemental leaven that is capable of making man human. It has thus cut itself off from the source of life, and inherited that wide emptiness which it named modern life. This starved degree of existence society had long considered to be life, until suddenly its hard crust fell in pieces and the world sank, darkened by the death of war. The fire of life was turned to consume life. The gifts of life crumbled before society. The Artist and the Poet departed from it. So that society inherits the fruits of its attitude. Its denial of the attributes of growth, which exist within Art and Religion; and its denial of the perceptions of the Fool in not allowing him a place within the form of the society of men and women, has, with other things, led inevitably to the death of a world where life is dissected in a fever of activities which grind to nothingness all human sensibility, together with those human faculties of communion, those sensitive organs of perception, evolved with great difficulty and patience; developed through long periods of struggle, through solitude and neglect; those perceptions of being, through which alone the nature of life can be lived and realized. So with the instruments of the realization of life thus silenced, society is left to pursue its existence. But existence is not life; when life begins existence ceases. When existence becomes illuminated it becomes life. It becomes illuminated through the charity of the Saint, which is the flowing of a wisdom perpetually washing society clean. It becomes illuminated by the Artist through the wisdom of beauty. It becomes illuminated by the Fool, the presence of whose very being brings back to society that ancient, original innocence in which the eternal music of life reveals the vibrations of its harmony. This innocence is part of the structure of a human society. Long sought after by penetrating spirits, denied, and put to death, by the mechanical animality in mankind; like the charity of the Saint, and the vision of the Artist, this innocence is above the speculations of philosophy; and the clever gymnastics of the intellect; it is unreachable by them, it is unknowable to them. It cannot be netted or catalogued by Science, nor can it be attained by intellectual achievement. It remains, however, the treasure of life, the healing of the wounds, the secret touch that gives strength, the elegant sorrow that understands the incomprehensible needs of the heart.

Deep in the anatomy of the Fool you will see the workings of that suffering which generates his lucid and life-giving gaiety. The suffering of the Fool is the golden material which, by the alchemy of his attitude towards life, is transmuted into the potent magic of his folly.

The Fool is not a revolutionist. He is not a reformer, and has no desire to reform society. Because he transforms it by the existence of his being, by the quality of his attitude. For the Fool is pure being, and, where that is existence becomes life. Through the Fool society again becomes connected with its source. In the Fool, society can embrace the origins of life, which it has forgotten and remains divided from, because of its hypnotized immersion in the habits of its world of machines. But among the roar and the wailing of their machines, the society of men sometimes senses an indefinable loss, a shadow, and for a moment, feels the absence of life.

A time will come when men and women will welcome the Fool among them. Because they will recognize in the Fool's naked face vividly imprinted, the image of life. Ultimately, it is the heart that searches and discovers life; because only that which has life can find life. And the human heart long ago recognized the Fool. That intense magic of life which is focused in the centres of Art and Religion, and for which most human beings secretly or openly long, shines in the clear emblem of the Fool's face. For the Fool is the servant of the heart.

There are no words to speak of the Fool. Words cannot express the Fool nor reveal his nature. One can only hint, give indirect clues, and hope that in spite of the more superficial discursive medium of words something may be conveyed about his attitude and sense of life. How can one express something so mobile, so near to the essence of life, with its perpetual flowing changes, as the Fool's nature? It needs profounder ways of communication than words in order to do this.

That is why I gladly turn to my painting to speak more deeply of the Fool.

Acknowledgements

There are a number of people to whom I am indebted for their help in the making of this book. The support and generosity of Robin Baring and Peter Nahum at the outset gave me the confidence to proceed with the project. Along the way I had the valuable help of Genevieve Overy, Stephen Overy, John Carey and Jill Burrows. Clive Hicks, once again, gave freely of his time and generously allowed me to make full use of his photographic archives. But my deepest debt of gratitude is owed to the Kalliopeia Foundation, who made this publication possible. All these I now thank in the hope that the final outcome meets with their approval.

Grateful acknowledgement is also made to the following for permission to reproduce the plates from works in their collection: Art Gallery of New South Wales, 22; Birmingham Museums & Art Gallery, 2; Bolton Museums & Art Gallery, 3; British Council Collection, 6 and 7; Colchester and Ipswich Museum Service, 25; The Fitzwilliam Museum, 1; Clive Hicks, 17, 18, 26 and rear cover; Hunterian Museum & Art Gallery, 5; Peter Nahum, front cover, 12, 14; Pallant House Gallery, 16; Sotheby's, 8, 19, 20, and page 32; Tate Gallery, 22, 23, 32; Wakefield Art Gallery, 11, 15; Offer Waterman & Co., 9, 10; The Whitworth Art Gallery, dedication page; Wolseley Fine Arts, 13.